How to Pass

English for Business

Preliminary Level

4TH EDITION

How to Pass English for Business Preliminary Level

4th Edition 2020

ISBN 978-3-922514-27-5

Published by: **Logophon Verlag GmbH**
Hauptstraße 23, 63811 Stockstadt am Main, Germany
Tel: 0 60 27 / 41 88 820
Fax: 0 60 27 / 41 88 40
E-mail: verlag@logophon.de
Website: www.logophon.de

In cooperation with: **LCCIEB Germany**
Platanenstr. 5, 07549 Gera
Tel: 0365 / 7 38 85 19
Fax: 0365 / 7 38 85 36
E-mail: info@lccieb-germany.com
Website: www.lccieb-germany.com

OTHER BUSINESS ENGLISH TITLES PUBLISHED BY LOGOPHON VERLAG GMBH:

How to Pass English for Business Level 1	ISBN 3-922514-28-6
How to Pass English for Business Level 2	ISBN 3-922514-29-4
How to Pass English for Business Level 3	ISBN 3-922514-32-4
How to Pass Spoken English for Industry and Commerce Preliminary Level	
Student's Book	ISBN 3-922514-33-2
Picture Book	ISBN 3-922514-39-1
How to Pass Spoken English for Industry and Commerce Level 2 (Threshold)	
Student's Book	ISBN 3-922514-34-0
Teacher's Book	ISBN 3-922514-40-5
Picture Book	ISBN 3-922514-42-1
How to Pass Spoken English for Industry and Commerce Level 3 (Intermediate)	
Student's Book	ISBN 3-922514-35-9
Teacher's Book	ISBN 3-922514-43-x
How to Pass Spoken English for Industry and Commerce Level 4 (Advanced)	
Student's Book	ISBN 3-922514-36-7
Teacher's Book	ISBN 3-922514-45-6
Business English Tests	ISBN 3-922514-91-x
More Business English Tests	ISBN 3-922514-92-8
Advanced Business English Tests	ISBN 3-922514-93-6

CONTENTS

Introduction

This book can be used either as a class book or for self-study. It contains 5 sections covering each of the tasks which appear in the London Chamber of Commerce and Industry Examinations Board's English for Business Preliminary Level examination. These tasks are:

- Multiple Choice
- Short Answers
- True/False
- Full Sentence Answers
- Message Writing

Each section has an introduction which explains how to approach the question. The approach consists of four stages which are:

1. Identify the task
2. How to answer
3. Now answer the questions
4. Check your work

In each section one completed example is provided in which all four stages are completed. A second example is given and students complete the four stages in the space provided. Six further practice questions follow. When students have completed all sections of the book they can attempt the 'REVISION TEST' which uses the completed examples from each section and revises each of the exam tasks in a random order. The 'FURTHER PRACTICE' section provides 10 new questions. Answers to all questions are contained at the back of the book. The 'GLOSSARY' section at the back lists the main words used in the book.

Two complete examination papers are included in the book. The first is at the beginning to show students what the exam looks like as a whole and how the individual exam tasks are linked. The second is at the end to provide a mock examination which can be carried out under exam conditions. Answers are provided at the back of the book.

Note to Teachers

The English for Business Preliminary Level examination lasts for one and a half hours. It consists of three sections and candidates must answer ALL questions. Section A contains a picture followed by fifteen multiple choice questions and ten short answer questions. Section B contains a dialogue followed by eleven true / false questions and eight questions requiring full sentence answers. Section C requires candidates to produce a short text, eg a memo, telephone message, based on the dialogue in section B and additional numerical information provided, eg price list, timetable.

A syllabus for the English for Business Preliminary Level examination and past papers are available from:

Education Development International PLC
LCCI International Qualifications
International House – Siskin Parkway East – Middlemarch Business Park
Coventry CV3 4PE – UK
www.ediplc.com

This book is the official LCCIEB examination preparation book for English for Business Preliminary Level. It contains authentic examination questions and has been reviewed by the LCCIEB Chief Examiner for English for Business Preliminary Level.

Section	Examiner's Use Only
A	
B	
C	
Total	

SAMPLE EXAMINATION PAPER 1

LCCI EXAMINATIONS BOARD

ENGLISH FOR BUSINESS

PRELIMINARY LEVEL

(Code No: 1044)

Instructions to Candidates

*(a) The time allowed for this examination is **1½** hours.*

*(b) Answer all **3** sections.*

(c) Use the spaces provided in the combined question and answer booklet to complete the answers. If more space is needed for answers or rough notes, use the supplementary sheets provided and secure them inside your booklet with your name and candidate number clearly written on each sheet. Rough notes should be clearly crossed through.

(d) Credit will be given for correct spelling, punctuation and grammar.

(e) Adequate and appropriate communication is required rather than a particular number of words.

(f) When you finish, check your work carefully.

(g) The use of standard English dictionaries and cordless non-programmable calculators is permitted. Candidates whose first language is not English may use a bilingual dictionary.

ENTER DETAILS BELOW

CANDIDATE'S NAME IN FULL
as it is to appear on the certificate **IDENTITY CARD NUMBER** ....

Subject Code Number ....**1044**.................................

Candidate's Number .... Centre Code ....

Full Private Address ....

.... Postcode ....

Centre Name and Address ....

....

STATE HERE THE NUMBER OF ADDITIONAL SHEETS HANDED IN [ ]

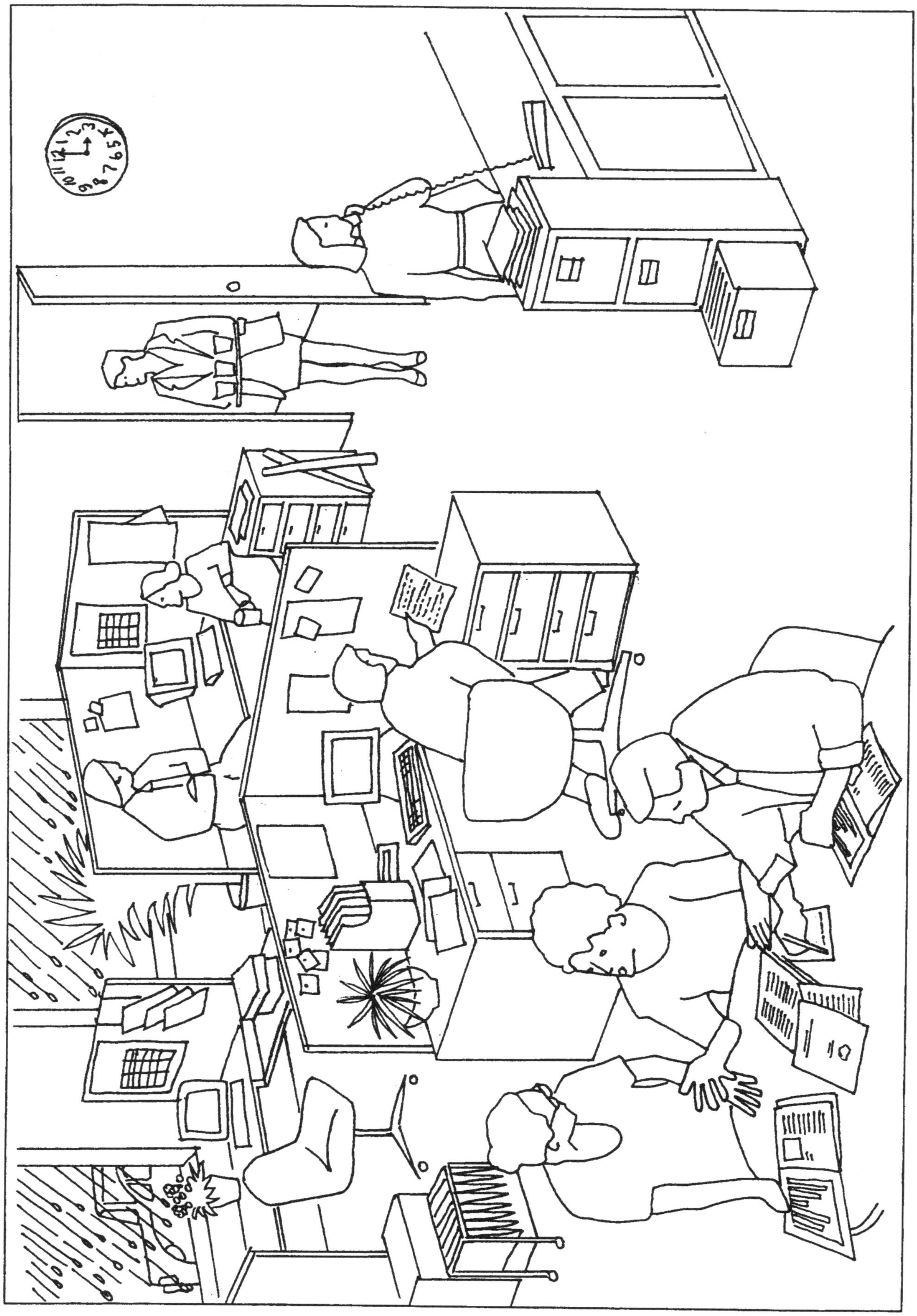

Section A

Look at the picture. Put a tick (✓) in the box for the best answer to each question.

A1 Is this a picture of (1 mark)

(a) a busy office? ☐

(b) a quiet office? ☐

(c) an empty office? ☐

A2 What time is it in the picture? (1 mark)

(a) one o'clock ☐

(b) three o'clock ☐

(c) five o'clock ☐

A3 A woman is speaking on the telephone. Is she (1 mark)

(a) sitting? ☐

(b) standing? ☐

(c) walking? ☐

A4 How many empty chairs can you see? (1 mark)

(a) none ☐

(b) one ☐

(c) two ☐

A5 A man is sitting and holding a paper in his left hand. Is he (1 mark)

(a) on the right of the picture? ☐

(b) on the left of the picture? ☐

(c) in the middle of the picture? ☐

A6 Where is the large plant? (1 mark)

(a) near the window ☐

(b) on a desk ☐

(c) next to a filing cabinet ☐

CONTINUED ON NEXT PAGE

SECTION A CONTINUED

A7 A woman at the front of the picture is talking. Who is on her left? (1 mark)

(a) a woman standing ☐

(b) a man speaking ☐

(c) a man writing ☐

A8 What shape is the clock? (1 mark)

(a) round ☐

(b) square ☐

(c) flat ☐

A9 Who is entering the room? (1 mark)

(a) a woman carrying a tea tray ☐

(b) a man drinking tea ☐

(c) a man eating cake ☐

A10 Which of these are **not** in the picture? (1 mark)

(a) filing cabinets ☐

(b) telephones ☐

(c) wastepaper baskets ☐

A11 Where is the clock? (1 mark)

(a) near the door ☐

(b) near the window ☐

(c) near a computer ☐

A12 Which desk only has a computer on it? (1 mark)

(a) the desk nearest the window ☐

(b) the desk in the middle ☐

(c) the desk nearest the door ☐

SECTION A CONTINUED

A13 How many people are sitting? (1 mark)

(a) three ☐

(b) five ☐

(c) eight ☐

A14 What are the windows made of? (1 mark)

(a) wood and glass ☐

(b) glass and paper ☐

(c) wood and metal ☐

A15 What time of day is it? (1 mark)

(a) morning ☐

(b) afternoon ☐

(c) night ☐

Look at the picture. Then write short answers to these questions where it says Answer.

A16 A woman has come into the office. Is she inside or outside the room? (2 marks)

Answer ______________________________

A17 A man is talking to a woman. Where is he sitting? (2 marks)

Answer ______________________________

A18 One man is writing with a pen. Which hand is he using? (2 marks)

Answer ______________________________

A19 What is the weather like outside the office? (2 marks)

Answer ______________________________

A20 Is the door open or is it closed? (2 marks)

Answer ______________________________

A21 How many computers are there in the office? (2 marks)

Answer ______________________________

CONTINUED ON NEXT PAGE

SECTION A CONTINUED

A22 Are there more men or more women in the office? (2 marks)

Answer ______________________________________

A23 A man is sitting at a desk facing the door. What is he doing? (2 marks)

Answer ______________________________________

A24 Who is wearing glasses? (2 marks)

Answer ______________________________________

A25 How many people can you see in the office? (2 marks)

Answer ______________________________________

(Total 35 marks)

SECTION B

Karen Duval is a secretary in a company called *Speedy Repairs*, based in the town of Newbridge. The company repairs electrical equipment. Karen is speaking on the telephone to a man called Parajit Singh.

Karen:	Good morning, Speedy Repairs, Karen speaking. Can I help you?
Mr Singh:	I hope you can. My name is Parajit Singh. Someone from your company came to my house yesterday because my television was broken. It had no sound. The repairman said he had mended the television but it is still not working.
Karen:	Is there still no sound?
Mr Singh:	Well, there is sound so we can listen to the television. But we can't watch it. It now has no picture.
Karen:	Oh dear!
Mr Singh:	My children and I wanted to watch the television last night because our favourite movie, *Titanic*, was on. We were very disappointed when we could not watch it.
Karen:	What is the name of the repairman?
Mr Singh:	I can't remember his name. He was a tall man and he was wearing glasses.
Karen:	What's your address, Mr Singh?
Mr Singh:	I live at 56 Central Drive in Newbridge.
Karen:	I'll check the name of the repairman who visited you and ask him to visit you again. All our repair staff are working now but I will give him a message when he returns to the office tonight. Will you be at home tomorrow morning?
Mr Singh:	I will be at work but my wife will be at home until 11.30.
Karen:	I'll make sure he visits your house tomorrow. I'm sorry about this, Mr Singh.
Mr Singh:	Thanks for your help. Goodbye.

Read these sentences about the conversation. Some are true and some are false. Put a tick (✓) in the TRUE or FALSE box.

		TRUE	FALSE	
B1	Karen Duval works for Speedy Repairs.	☐	☐	(1 mark)
B2	Mr Singh is visiting Speedy Repairs.	☐	☐	(1 mark)
B3	Speedy Repairs mends broken electrical equipment.	☐	☐	(1 mark)
B4	Mr Singh is a father.	☐	☐	(1 mark)

SECTION B CONTINUED

		TRUE	FALSE	
B5	Karen is going to ask someone to visit Mr Singh's house.	☐	☐	(1 mark)
B6	None of the repair staff are working now.	☐	☐	(1 mark)
B7	Mr Singh wanted to watch television last night.	☐	☐	(1 mark)
B8	Karen's address is 56 Central Drive, Newbridge.	☐	☐	(1 mark)
B9	Mr Singh cannot remember the name of the repairman.	☐	☐	(1 mark)
B10	Mr Singh's television now has no sound.	☐	☐	(1 mark)
B11	Mr Singh thanks Karen for her help.	☐	☐	(1 mark)

Write a sentence to answer each question about the conversation on the line marked Answer.

B12 What time of day is it when Karen speaks to Mr Singh? (3 marks)

Answer ______________________________

B13 What is Karen's job? (3 marks)

Answer ______________________________

B14 What did the repairman who visited Mr Singh look like? (3 marks)

Answer ______________________________

B15 Where will Mr Singh be tomorrow morning? (3 marks)

Answer ______________________________

B16 What is the favourite movie of Mr Singh's family? (3 marks)

Answer ______________________________

B17 When will Mr Singh's wife be at home tomorrow? (3 marks)

Answer ______________________________

B18 Where is the company *Speedy Repairs* based? (3 marks)

Answer ______________________________

B19 What is now wrong with Mr Singh's television? (3 marks)

Answer ______________________________

(Total 35 marks)

OVER

SECTION C

Read the conversation between Karen and Mr Singh and then look at the list of the addresses visited by repair staff yesterday.

Repair person	Addresses visited
Les Fisher	19 Northern Street Flat C Vulcan Towers 318b Oak Street
Pat Wagner	24 Glebe Road 56 Central Drive 4 Railway Street 13 Menin Road
Vic McTeer	19 Baker Drive 46 Silver Street 3 Avon Street
Jan Heymann	58 London Road 173 Park Avenue

Use the information to give a message on the **memo** form below to the repairman who visited Mr Singh yesterday.

MEMORANDUM

To: ______________________________ Date: _________________

From: ____________________________

Subject: ____

(30 marks)

SECTIONS
1 – 5

SECTION 1: MULTIPLE CHOICE

STAGE 1: IDENTIFY THE TASK

The multiple choice questions appear in Section A of the examination and are based on the picture provided for Section A. You have to look at the picture, read each question and decide which of the three answers given is the best answer. There are 15 questions and each question is worth 1 mark. The instruction normally reads "Look at the picture. Put a tick (✓) in the box for the best answer to each question".

STAGE 2: HOW TO ANSWER

- Look at the picture.
- Read each question carefully.
- Read answers (a), (b) and (c) carefully.
- Check the picture again.

Remember:

- If you can't answer a question, leave it and come back to it later.

STAGE 3: NOW ANSWER THE QUESTIONS

- Choose the **best** answer.
- Put a tick in the appropriate box.

STAGE 4: CHECK YOUR WORK

- Have you chosen the **best** answer?
- Have you answered all the questions?

COMPLETED EXAMPLE

Look at the picture. Put a tick (✓) in the box for the best answer to each question.

STAGE 1: IDENTIFY THE TASK

Put a tick (✓) in the box for the best answer to each question.

STAGE 2: HOW TO ANSWER

- Have you looked at the picture? ✓
- Have you read each question carefully? ✓
- Have you read answers (a), (b) and (c) carefully? ✓
- Have you checked the picture again? ✓

STAGE 3: NOW ANSWER THE QUESTIONS

1 What is this room? (1 mark)

(a) a factory ☐
(b) a restaurant ☐
(c) an office ☑

2 What time of day is it? (1 mark)

(a) morning ☑
(b) afternoon ☐
(c) night ☐

3 What is the weather outside the room? (1 mark)

(a) it is sunny ☐
(b) it is raining ☑
(c) it is cold ☐

4	**A man is sitting facing the door. What is he wearing?**		(1 mark)
	(a) a checked shirt	☑	
	(b) a striped shirt	☐	
	(c) a black shirt	☐	
5	**What can you not see in the picture?**		(1 mark)
	(a) a filing cabinet	☐	
	(b) a telephone	☐	
	(c) a briefcase	☑	
6	**Who is walking?**		(1 mark)
	(a) the man carrying a box	☑	
	(b) the woman speaking on the telephone	☐	
	(c) the man writing	☐	
7	**Who is wet?**		(1 mark)
	(a) the man outside the room	☐	
	(b) the man coming into the room	☑	
	(c) the man going out of the room	☐	
8	**What shape is the clock?**		(1 mark)
	(a) square	☐	
	(b) rectangular	☐	
	(c) round	☑	
9	**A man is carrying a box. Is it in**		(1 mark)
	(a) his left hand?	☐	
	(b) his right hand?	☐	
	(c) both hands?	☑	
10	**What is on the desk nearest the door?**		(1 mark)
	(a) a telephone	☐	
	(b) a computer	☑	
	(c) a wastepaper bin	☐	
11	**What is the woman with long hair doing?**		(1 mark)
	(a) using the fax machine	☑	
	(b) drinking a coffee	☐	
	(c) carrying a briefcase	☐	
12	**How many men are writing?**		(1 mark)
	(a) none	☐	
	(b) one	☑	
	(c) three	☐	
13	**A man is sitting at the desk on the right. Has he**		(1 mark)
	(a) long hair?	☐	
	(b) short hair?	☐	
	(c) no hair?	☑	
14	**What is between the door and the window?**		(1 mark)
	(a) a clock	☐	
	(b) a filing cabinet	☐	
	(c) a clock and a filing cabinet	☑	
15	**One desk has nothing on it. Where is it?**		(1 mark)
	(a) near a window	☑	
	(b) next to the door	☐	
	(c) outside the room	☐	

STAGE 4: CHECK YOUR WORK

- Have you chosen the **best** answer? ✓
- Have you answered all the questions? ✓

YOUR EXAMPLE

Look at the picture. Put a tick (✓) in the box for the best answer to each question.

STAGE 1: IDENTIFY THE TASK

....

STAGE 2: HOW TO ANSWER

- Have you looked at the picture? ☐
- Have you read each question carefully? ☐
- Have you read answers (a), (b) and (c) carefully? ☐
- Have you checked the picture again? ☐

STAGE 3: NOW ANSWER THE QUESTIONS

1 **What is this room?** (1 mark)
(a) a library ☐
(b) a factory ☐
(c) a reception area ☐

2 **How many computers are in the picture?** (1 mark)
(a) none ☐
(b) two ☐
(c) four ☐

3 **Where is the clock?** (1 mark)
(a) above the drinks machine ☐
(b) below the drinks machine ☐
(c) behind the drinks machine ☐

4 **What are the tables made of?** (1 mark)
(a) wood ☐
(b) glass ☐
(c) leather ☐

5 **What is on the filing cabinet?** (1 mark)
(a) files ☐
(b) books ☐
(c) nothing ☐

6 **Are there more women or more men in the picture?** (1 mark)
(a) women ☐
(b) men ☐
(c) the same number ☐

7 **A woman is wearing a flowered dress. Is she** (1 mark)
(a) sitting? ☐
(b) standing? ☐
(c) walking? ☐

8 **Which of these is not in the room?** (1 mark)
(a) a photocopier ☐
(b) a drinks machine ☐
(c) a wastepaper basket ☐

9 **What is between the filing cabinet and the door?** (1 mark)
(a) a window ☐
(b) a drinks machine ☐
(c) a computer ☐

10 **Which is the smallest?** (1 mark)
(a) a chair ☐
(b) a table ☐
(c) a filing cabinet ☐

11 **What time of day is it?** (1 mark)
(a) morning ☐
(b) afternoon ☐
(c) evening ☐

12 **What shape is the window?** (1 mark)
(a) round ☐
(b) square ☐
(c) rectangular ☐

13 **What can you see through the window?** (1 mark)
(a) an office ☐
(b) a car park ☐
(c) a park ☐

14 **Two women are standing and talking. What else are they doing?** (1 mark)
(a) eating ☐
(b) smoking ☐
(c) drinking ☐

15 **How many people are in the picture?** (1 mark)
(a) ten ☐
(b) twelve ☐
(c) thirteen ☐

STAGE 4: CHECK YOUR WORK

- Have you chosen the **best** answer? ☐
- Have you answered all the questions? ☐

PRACTICE 1

Look at the picture. Put a tick (✓) in the box for the best answer to each question.

1 What are some people in the picture doing? (1 mark)

(a) sleeping ☐
(b) waiting ☐
(c) lifting ☐

2 How many people are in the picture? (1 mark)

(a) twenty ☐
(b) eleven ☐
(c) none ☐

3 What time of day is it? (1 mark)

(a) night ☐
(b) evening ☐
(c) afternoon ☐

4 A man is coming into the room. What is he holding in his right hand? (1 mark)

(a) an umbrella ☐
(b) a briefcase ☐
(c) a cup of tea ☐

5 What is under one of the desks? (1 mark)

(a) a computer ☐
(b) a clock ☐
(c) a wastepaper bin ☐

6 Five people are standing together. What is the man in the middle doing? (1 mark)
(a) reading a newspaper ☐
(b) looking at his watch ☐
(c) talking ☐

7 Which of these does the room not have? (1 mark)
(a) stairs ☐
(b) a door ☐
(c) a window ☐

8 Two women are by desks in the picture. What are they doing? (1 mark)
(a) writing ☐
(b) sitting ☐
(c) speaking on the telephone ☐

9 A man and a woman are standing and talking. What is the woman carrying? (1 mark)
(a) an umbrella ☐
(b) a clock ☐
(c) a briefcase ☐

10 What is made of metal in the room? (1 mark)
(a) the coats ☐
(b) the window ☐
(c) the filing cabinets ☐

11 What is on the desk on the left of the coat stand? (1 mark)
(a) a computer ☐
(b) a telephone ☐
(c) a lamp ☐

12 A woman is speaking on the telephone. What is the man on her right doing? (1 mark)
(a) reading a newspaper ☐
(b) coming into the room ☐
(c) looking out of the window ☐

13 Who is wearing a hat? (1 mark)
(a) a man in front of the door ☐
(b) a woman outside the window ☐
(c) a woman near the door ☐

14 Are most of the people in the picture (1 mark)
(a) standing? ☐
(b) sitting? ☐
(c) walking? ☐

15 What do we call the five people standing together? (1 mark)
(a) a queue ☐
(b) a crowd ☐
(c) an audience ☐

PRACTICE 2

Look at the picture. Put a tick (✓) in the box for the best answer to each question.

1 How many people are in the picture? (1 mark)
(a) eight ☐
(b) nine ☐
(c) eleven ☐

2 What is above the bookshelves? (1 mark)
(a) a television ☐
(b) a table ☐
(c) a clock ☐

3 What is on the filing cabinet? (1 mark)
(a) a vase of flowers ☐
(b) files ☐
(c) nothing ☐

4 A man is standing next to the television. What is he doing? (1 mark)
(a) pointing at the television ☐
(b) speaking on the telephone ☐
(c) writing a report ☐

5 A man is coming into the room. What is he carrying? (1 mark)
(a) a book ☐
(b) an umbrella ☐
(c) a briefcase ☐

6 **What time is it?** (1 mark)
(a) one o'clock ☐
(b) two o'clock ☐
(c) three o'clock ☐

7 **How many chairs are empty?** (1 mark)
(a) none ☐
(b) one ☐
(c) six ☐

8 **A woman is writing. What is the man next to her doing?** (1 mark)
(a) drinking a glass of water ☐
(b) speaking on the telephone ☐
(c) going out of the room ☐

9 **Where is the small table?** (1 mark)
(a) outside the door ☐
(b) underneath the window ☐
(c) near the shelves ☐

10 **Who is looking at a watch?** (1 mark)
(a) the woman standing in the room ☐
(b) the man sitting at a table ☐
(c) the woman sitting at a table ☐

11 **How many windows are in the room?** (1 mark)
(a) one ☐
(b) two ☐
(c) three ☐

12 **What are most of the people doing?** (1 mark)
(a) standing ☐
(b) sitting ☐
(c) walking ☐

13 **Who is wearing a hat?** (1 mark)
(a) the man coming into the room ☐
(b) the man standing next to the TV ☐
(c) the woman sitting at a table ☐

14 **Where is the television in the picture?** (1 mark)
(a) on the right ☐
(b) on the left ☐
(c) in the middle ☐

15 **Describe the weather outside the room.** (1 mark)
(a) It is hot. ☐
(b) It is cold. ☐
(c) It is raining. ☐

PRACTICE 3

Look at the picture. Put a tick (✓) in the box for the best answer to each question.

1 How many people are in the picture? (1 mark)
- (a) three ☐
- (b) eleven ☐
- (c) twenty ☐

2 What time is it? (1 mark)
- (a) twelve o'clock ☐
- (b) ten o'clock ☐
- (c) one o'clock ☐

3 A man is on a ladder. What is he doing? (1 mark)
- (a) talking on the telephone ☐
- (b) painting the wall ☐
- (c) cleaning the clock ☐

4 What is broken? (1 mark)
- (a) the drinks machine ☐
- (b) the computer ☐
- (c) the telephone ☐

5 What is this room? (1 mark)
- (a) a reception area ☐
- (b) a bedroom ☐
- (c) a factory ☐

6 What is the door made of? (1 mark)
(a) paper ☐
(b) wood and glass ☐
(c) metal ☐

7 What is not in the picture? (1 mark)
(a) a computer ☐
(b) a telephone ☐
(c) a filing cabinet ☐

8 What shape is the clock? (1 mark)
(a) triangular ☐
(b) round ☐
(c) square ☐

**9 Two people are working at the back of the room.
What is the area where they work in called?** (1 mark)
(a) a store ☐
(b) a factory ☐
(c) a theatre ☐

10 A man has just received a box. What is he saying? (1 mark)
(a) "Good afternoon." ☐
(b) "Hello." ☐
(c) "Thank you." ☐

11 Does the room look (1 mark)
(a) quiet? ☐
(b) empty? ☐
(c) busy? ☐

12 How many chairs do not have people sitting on them? (1 mark)
(a) one ☐
(b) two ☐
(c) none ☐

13 Is the door (1 mark)
(a) open? ☐
(b) closed? ☐
(c) half-open? ☐

14 Where are some books? (1 mark)
(a) on top of the desk ☐
(b) on a shelf ☐
(c) in a cupboard ☐

15 How many women are sitting? (1 mark)
(a) none ☐
(b) eleven ☐
(c) two ☐

PRACTICE 4

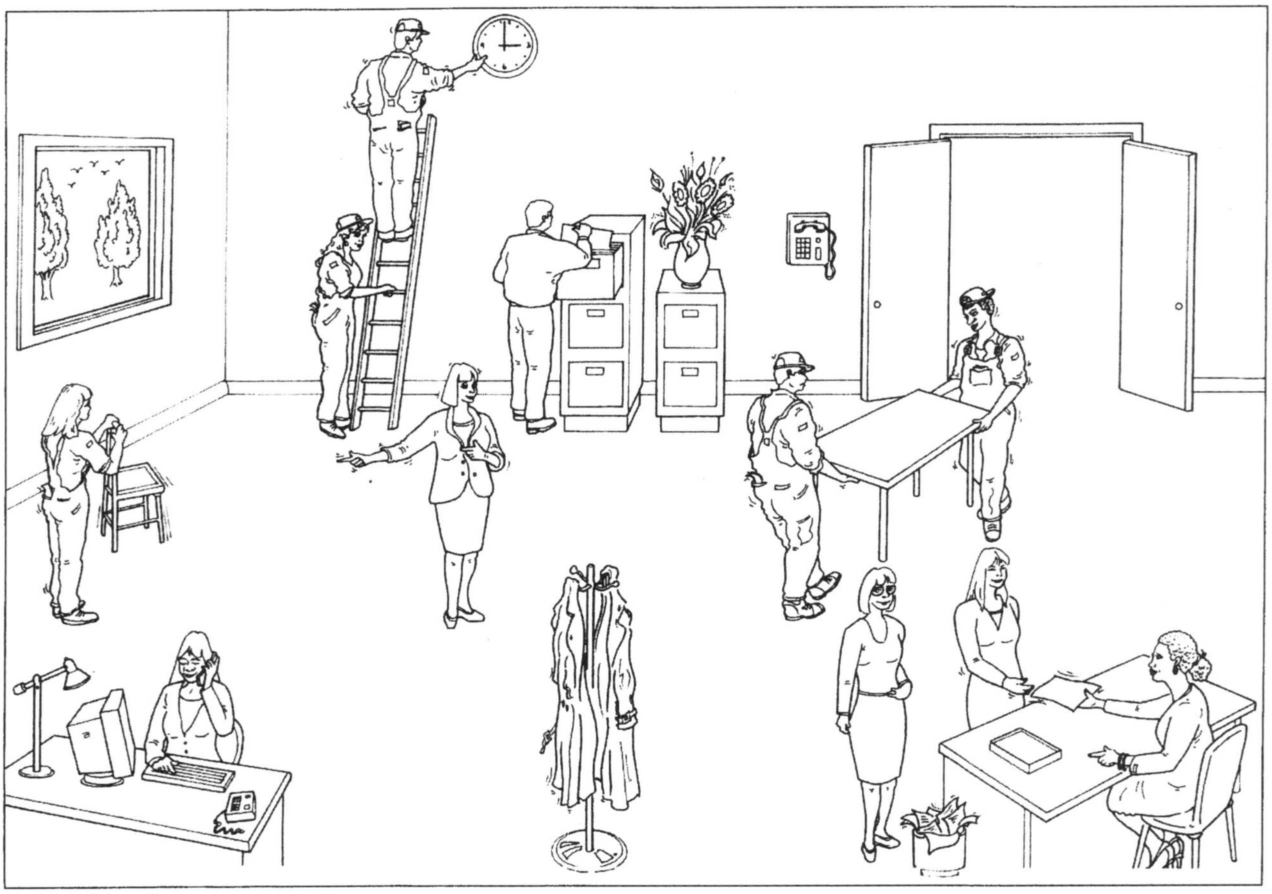

Look at the picture. Put a tick (✓) in the box for the best answer to each question.

1 Is this picture (1 mark)
- (a) an office? ☐
- (b) a house? ☐
- (c) a factory? ☐

2 How many people are in the picture? (1 mark)
- (a) none ☐
- (b) nine ☐
- (c) eleven ☐

3 How many people are sitting? (1 mark)
- (a) two ☐
- (b) five ☐
- (c) eleven ☐

4 A woman is sitting at a desk on the right of the picture. What is she doing? (1 mark)
- (a) giving a paper to a man ☐
- (b) giving a paper to a woman ☐
- (c) drinking a cup of tea ☐

5 What is under the window? (1 mark)
- (a) a table ☐
- (b) a clock ☐
- (c) nothing ☐

6 **A woman is holding a chair. What is it made of?** (1 mark)
(a) paper ☐
(b) glass ☐
(c) wood ☐

7 **How long is the ladder?** (1 mark)
(a) about 1 metre ☐
(b) about 3 metres ☐
(c) about 10 metres ☐

8 **Is the wastepaper bin** (1 mark)
(a) full? ☐
(b) empty? ☐
(c) half-empty? ☐

9 **Who is wearing glasses?** (1 mark)
(a) the woman standing near a desk ☐
(b) the man standing near a ladder ☐
(c) no-one ☐

10 **What is next to the computer on the desk?** (1 mark)
(a) a lamp ☐
(b) a book ☐
(c) a pencil ☐

11 **A man is looking in a drawer in a filing cabinet.**
Which drawer is he looking in? (1 mark)
(a) bottom drawer ☐
(b) middle drawer ☐
(c) top drawer ☐

12 **What is between the smaller filing cabinet and the door?** (1 mark)
(a) a large filing cabinet ☐
(b) a window ☐
(c) a telephone ☐

13 **Who is using a pen?** (1 mark)
(a) a man ☐
(b) a woman ☐
(c) no-one ☐

14 **A man is on a ladder. What is he holding?** (1 mark)
(a) a clock ☐
(b) a desk ☐
(c) a chair ☐

15 **Which of these is not in the picture?** (1 mark)
(a) a coat stand ☐
(b) a bed ☐
(c) a clock ☐

PRACTICE 5

Look at the picture. Put a tick (✓) in the box for the best answer to each question.

1 How many people are in the room? (1 mark)
- (a) one ☐
- (b) four ☐
- (c) six ☐

2 How many people are standing? (1 mark)
- (a) none ☐
- (b) two ☐
- (c) four ☐

3 Where is the calendar? (1 mark)
- (a) above the filing cabinet ☐
- (b) under the filing cabinet ☐
- (c) between the filing cabinet and the window ☐

4 What is on the filing cabinet? (1 mark)
- (a) a vase of flowers ☐
- (b) a picture ☐
- (c) a calendar ☐

5 Who is wearing glasses? (1 mark)
- (a) the man looking out of the window ☐
- (b) the man pointing at the clock ☐
- (c) the woman wearing a hat ☐

6 What is outside the window? (1 mark)
(a) a tree ☐
(b) a house ☐
(c) an office block ☐

7 What time is it? (1 mark)
(a) afternoon ☐
(b) ten o'clock ☐
(c) mid-day ☐

8 How many desks are next to a wall? (1 mark)
(a) none ☐
(b) one ☐
(c) two ☐

9 Where is the telephone? (1 mark)
(a) on the small desk ☐
(b) on the large desk ☐
(c) on the floor ☐

10 Who is carrying a briefcase? (1 mark)
(a) the woman coming into the room ☐
(b) the man with the glasses ☐
(c) the man pointing at the clock ☐

11 How many chairs are in the room? (1 mark)
(a) none ☐
(b) two ☐
(c) four ☐

12 What is this room? (1 mark)
(a) an office ☐
(b) a reception area ☐
(c) a factory ☐

13 Where is the computer? (1 mark)
(a) under the desk ☐
(b) on the desk ☐
(c) next to the desk ☐

14 What is the filing cabinet made of? (1 mark)
(a) paper ☐
(b) glass ☐
(c) metal ☐

15 A man is pointing at the clock. Does he look (1 mark)
(a) happy? ☐
(b) angry? ☐
(c) pleased? ☐

PRACTICE 6

Look at the picture. Put a tick (✓) in the box for the best answer to each question.

1 What is the picture? (1 mark)
(a) inside an office building ☐
(b) a street outside an office building ☐
(c) outside a factory ☐

2 What time is it in the picture? (1 mark)
(a) twelve o'clock ☐
(b) five o'clock ☐
(c) seven o'clock ☐

3 How many people are inside the office building? (1 mark)
(a) none ☐
(b) seven ☐
(c) sixteen ☐

4 A woman is in the car. What is she doing? (1 mark)
(a) driving the car ☐
(b) talking on the telephone ☐
(c) pointing at the office building ☐

5 A man with a hat is outside. Where is he going? (1 mark)
(a) away from the office building ☐
(b) towards the office building ☐
(c) into the office building ☐

6 Which is tallest? (1 mark)
(a) the office building ☐
(b) the shops ☐
(c) the tree ☐

7 What shape is the clock? (1 mark)
(a) round ☐
(b) square ☐
(c) rectangular ☐

8 What is in the street next to the two women? (1 mark)
(a) a car ☐
(b) a telephone box ☐
(c) a tree ☐

9 How many shops are in the picture? (1 mark)
(a) none ☐
(b) one ☐
(c) two ☐

10 What are the windows made of? (1 mark)
(a) leather ☐
(b) glass ☐
(c) cotton ☐

11 Where is the tree? (1 mark)
(a) between the office building and the shops ☐
(b) inside the office building ☐
(c) next to a door ☐

12 How many floors does the office building have? (1 mark)
(a) one ☐
(b) two ☐
(c) three ☐

13 A woman has come out of a shop. What does this shop sell? (1 mark)
(a) books ☐
(b) furniture ☐
(c) fruit and vegetables ☐

14 Where is a woman using a computer? (1 mark)
(a) inside the office building ☐
(b) near the office building ☐
(c) on top of the office building ☐

15 Is the weather in the picture (1 mark)
(a) sunny? ☐
(b) raining? ☐
(c) cold? ☐

SECTION 2: SHORT ANSWERS

STAGE 1: IDENTIFY THE TASK

The short answer questions appear in Section A of the examination and are based on the picture provided for Section A. You have to look at the picture and write a short answer to each question. There are 10 questions and each question is worth 2 marks. The instruction normally reads “Look at the picture. Then write **short answers** to these questions where it says Answer”.

STAGE 2: HOW TO ANSWER

- Look at the picture.
- Read each question carefully.
- Check the picture again.

Remember:

- If you can’t answer a question, leave it and come back to it later.
- Your answer must be **short.**

STAGE 3: NOW ANSWER THE QUESTIONS

- Write a **short** answer to the question where it says Answer.

Remember:

- Do not write a full sentence.
- A short answer is one word, a number, a time or a phrase.

  Examples

  Answer: “morning”

  Answer: “four”

  Answer: “seven o’clock”

  Answer: “using a computer”

STAGE 4: CHECK YOUR WORK

- Have you answered all the questions?
- Are your answers **short**?
- Have you checked your spelling?

COMPLETED EXAMPLE

Look at the picture. Then write short answers to these questions where it says Answer.

STAGE 1: IDENTIFY THE TASK

Write short answers to the questions where it says Answer.

STAGE 2: HOW TO ANSWER

• Have you looked at the picture?	✓
• Have you read each question carefully?	✓
• Have you checked the picture again?	✓

STAGE 3: NOW ANSWER THE QUESTIONS

1	There are two buildings in the picture. How many people can you see inside the small building?	
Answer:	**three**	(2 marks)
2	What time is it in the picture?	
Answer:	**one o'clock**	(2 marks)
3	Where can you see a woman using a computer?	
Answer:	**inside the small building**	(2 marks)
4	Where is the dog in the picture?	
Answer:	**between the buildings**	(2 marks)
5	A man and a woman are standing in front of the small building. What is the man doing?	
Answer:	**giving the woman a letter**	(2 marks)
6	What can you see flying in the sky?	
Answer:	**an aeroplane**	(2 marks)
7	Which is parked at the side of the road, the car or the van?	
Answer:	**the van**	(2 marks)
8	In a room of the large building a man is speaking to a woman. What is she doing?	
Answer:	**writing**	(2 marks)
9	How many windows can you see in the large building?	
Answer:	**five**	(2 marks)
10	What time of day is it in the picture?	
Answer:	**afternoon**	(2 marks)

STAGE 4: CHECK YOUR WORK

• Have you answered all the questions?	✓
• Are your answers **short**?	✓
• Have you checked your spelling?	✓

YOUR EXAMPLE

Look at the picture. Then write short answers to these questions where it says Answer.

STAGE 1: IDENTIFY THE TASK

....

STAGE 2: HOW TO ANSWER

- Have you looked at the picture?
- Have you read each question carefully?
- Have you checked the picture again?

STAGE 3: NOW ANSWER THE QUESTIONS

1	What time is it in the picture?	
Answer:		(2 marks)
2	A woman is writing. Which hand is she using?	
Answer:		(2 marks)
3	What is the woman in front of the desk wearing?	
Answer:		(2 marks)
4	A man is sitting near a small table. What is he doing?	
Answer:		(2 marks)
5	A woman is also sitting near the small table. What is she doing?	
Answer:		(2 marks)
6	What is outside the windows?	
Answer:		(2 marks)
7	A woman is sitting next to a window. What is she doing?	
Answer:		(2 marks)
8	A woman is speaking on the telephone. Where is she standing?	
Answer:		(2 marks)
9	How many people are in the picture?	
Answer:		(2 marks)
10	Where is there a tree in the room?	
Answer:		(2 marks)

STAGE 4: CHECK YOUR WORK

- Have you answered all the questions? ☐
- Are your answers **short**? ☐
- Have you checked your spelling? ☐

PRACTICE 1

Look at the picture. Then write short answers to these questions where it says Answer.

1	What is between the stairs and the filing cabinets?	
Answer:		(2 marks)
2	One woman is sitting at the desk on the left. What is she doing?	
Answer:		(2 marks)
3	A man wearing glasses is talking to a woman. What is she doing?	
Answer:		(2 marks)
4	How many women are sitting on chairs?	
Answer:		(2 marks)
5	There are two filing cabinets. What is on top of the cabinet on the right?	
Answer:		(2 marks)
6	What time is it?	
Answer:		(2 marks)
7	Where is the woman with the briefcase?	
Answer:		(2 marks)
8	Are all the men standing?	
Answer:		(2 marks)
9	A woman is holding a cup of coffee. In which hand is she holding it?	
Answer:		(2 marks)
10	Is the door open or closed?	
Answer:		(2 marks)

PRACTICE 2

Look at the picture. Then write short answers to these questions where it says Answer.

1	What is between the shelves and the filing cabinet?	
Answer:		(2 marks)
2	A woman is sitting at a desk. What is she using?	
Answer:		(2 marks)
3	How many women are in the picture?	
Answer:		(2 marks)
4	Is the door closed?	
Answer:		(2 marks)
5	What time is it?	
Answer:		(2 marks)
6	A woman is holding a mobile telephone. Is it in her right or left hand?	
Answer:		(2 marks)
7	What is under the desk?	
Answer:		(2 marks)
8	Where is the window?	
Answer:		(2 marks)
9	A man wearing a hat is giving something to another man. What is it?	
Answer:		(2 marks)
10	What is on the desk to the woman's left?	
Answer:		(2 marks)

PRACTICE 3

Look at the picture. Then write short answers to these questions where it says Answer.

1 What time is it in the picture?	
Answer:	(2 marks)
2 How many bookcases are in the picture?	
Answer:	(2 marks)
3 What is the older man doing?	
Answer:	(2 marks)
4 Where is the small table?	
Answer:	(2 marks)
5 Who is sitting?	
Answer:	(2 marks)
6 What is outside the window?	
Answer:	(2 marks)
7 How many people are in the picture?	
Answer:	(2 marks)
8 Where is the vase of flowers?	
Answer:	(2 marks)
9 Who is coming into the room?	
Answer:	(2 marks)
10 Is there a telephone in the picture?	
Answer:	(2 marks)

PRACTICE 4

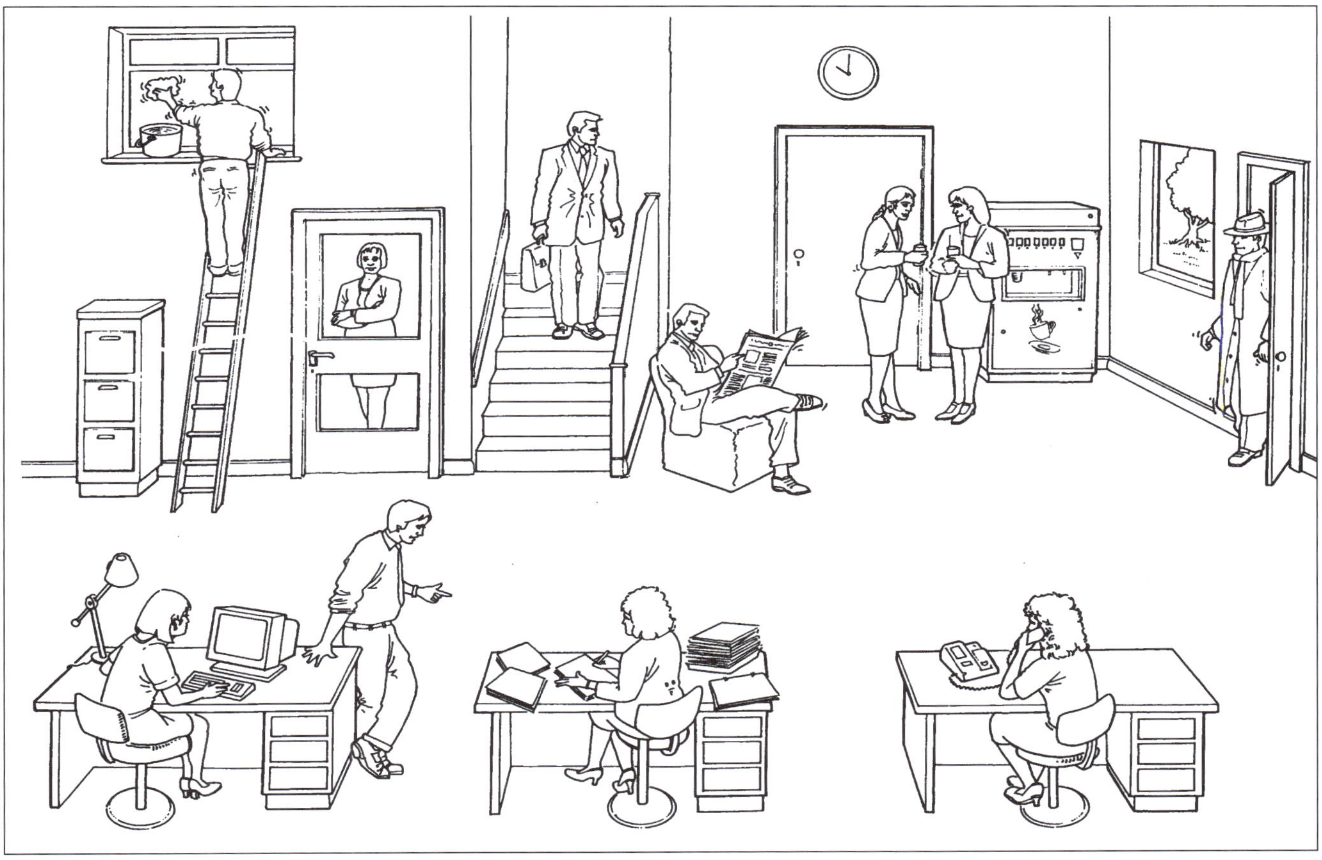

Look at the picture. Then write short answers to these questions where it says Answer.

1	How many desks are in the picture?	
Answer:		(2 marks)
2	Where is the clock?	
Answer:		(2 marks)
3	What is outside the window on the right?	
Answer:		(2 marks)
4	A man wearing a hat is in the picture. What is he doing?	
Answer:		(2 marks)
5	How many people are sitting on chairs?	
Answer:		(2 marks)
6	A man is coming down the stairs. What is he carrying?	
Answer:		(2 marks)
7	Are there more women or men in the picture?	
Answer:		(2 marks)
8	A woman is sitting at the middle desk. What is she doing?	
Answer:		(2 marks)
9	A young man is sitting next to the stairs. What is he reading?	
Answer:		(2 marks)
10	How many people are in the picture?	
Answer:		(2 marks)

PRACTICE 5

Look at the picture. Then write short answers to these questions where it says Answer.

1 How many people are in the picture?	
Answer:	(2 marks)
2 What time is it in the picture?	
Answer:	(2 marks)
3 What is the woman doing who is sitting nearest the door?	
Answer:	(2 marks)
4 What is between the window and the door?	
Answer:	(2 marks)
5 What is a woman bringing into the room?	
Answer:	(2 marks)
6 Who is wearing glasses?	
Answer:	(2 marks)
7 Is the door closed?	
Answer:	(2 marks)
8 With which hand is the woman writing?	
Answer:	(2 marks)
9 Are there more men or women in the picture?	
Answer:	(2 marks)
10 How many people are talking?	
Answer:	(2 marks)

PRACTICE 6

Look at the picture. Then write short answers to these questions where it says Answer.

1 Are most people in the picture talking?	
Answer:	(2 marks)
2 A man is outside the door. What is he doing?	
Answer:	(2 marks)
3 Is the door closed?	
Answer:	(2 marks)
4 What shape is the window?	
Answer:	(2 marks)
5 Two women and a man are sitting at a large table. Who is in the middle?	
Answer:	(2 marks)
6 A woman is sitting at a small desk. What is she doing?	
Answer:	(2 marks)
7 What is on the small table?	
Answer:	(2 marks)
8 A woman is sitting on the older man's left. What is she doing?	
Answer:	(2 marks)
9 A young man is wearing a jacket. What is he holding?	
Answer:	(2 marks)
10 Are there more men or women in the picture?	
Answer:	(2 marks)

SECTION 3: TRUE / FALSE

STAGE 1: IDENTIFY THE TASK

The true / false questions appear in Section B of the examination and are based on the conversation provided for Section B. You have to read the conversation, read each sentence and decide whether the sentence is true or false. There are 11 questions and each question is worth 1 mark. The instruction normally reads "Read these sentences about the conversation. Some are true and some are false. Put a tick (✓) in the TRUE or FALSE box".

STAGE 2: HOW TO ANSWER

- Read the conversation.
- Read each sentence carefully.
- Check the conversation again.

Remember:

- If you can't answer a question, leave it and come back to it later.

STAGE 3: NOW ANSWER THE QUESTIONS

- Put a tick in the appropriate box.

STAGE 4: CHECK YOUR WORK

- Have you answered all the questions?

COMPLETED EXAMPLE

Mr Robert Clifton is a manager of a business. He is ill today and not at work. Mrs Pauline Heston needs to speak to him. She is calling the business on the telephone and is speaking to Miss Laura Wilson.

Miss Wilson: Hello. This is Laura Wilson. Can I help you?

Mrs Heston: Good morning. My name is Pauline Heston. Can I speak to Mr Clifton, please?

Miss Wilson: I'm sorry, Mr Clifton is not here. He's at home.

Mrs Heston: When will he be at work? I need to speak to him. It's very important.

Miss Wilson: He's ill today, but he'll be here tomorrow.

Mrs Heston: Would you give him a message, please? I'd like to make an appointment to see him. I have something to tell him about the building he wants to buy in Australia.

Miss Wilson: I can make this appointment. I work with Mr Clifton and I have his diary.

Mrs Heston: I'd like to see him next week. I am free on Tuesday afternoon, Wednesday morning or Friday morning.

Miss Wilson: I'll look in his diary and see when he is free.

Mrs Heston: I'm going out now. Ask Mr Clifton to speak to me tomorrow to say when he can see me.

Miss Wilson: Of course, I'll speak to Mr Clifton.

Mrs Heston: Thank you very much for your help.

Miss Wilson: Goodbye, Mrs Heston.

Read these sentences about the conversation. Some are true and some are false. Put a tick (✓) in the TRUE or FALSE box.

STAGE 1: IDENTIFY THE TASK

Put a tick (✓) in the TRUE or FALSE box.

STAGE 2: HOW TO ANSWER

• Have you read the conversation?	✓
• Have you read each sentence carefully?	✓
• Have you checked the conversation again?	✓

STAGE 3: NOW ANSWER THE QUESTIONS

		TRUE	FALSE	
1	Mr Clifton is ill today.	☑	☐	(1 mark)
2	Mrs Heston is speaking to Miss Wilson.	☑	☐	(1 mark)
3	Mr Clifton is not at work today.	☑	☐	(1 mark)
4	Mrs Heston has Mr Clifton's diary.	☐	☑	(1 mark)
5	Miss Wilson's first name is Pauline.	☐	☑	(1 mark)
6	Mr Clifton will speak to Mrs Heston tomorrow.	☑	☐	(1 mark)
7	Miss Wilson is a colleague of Mr Clifton.	☑	☐	(1 mark)
8	Mrs Heston wants to buy a building in Australia.	☐	☑	(1 mark)
9	Miss Wilson wants to see Mr Clifton next week.	☐	☑	(1 mark)
10	Mrs Heston's message is very important.	☑	☐	(1 mark)
11	Mrs Heston is free on Tuesday morning next week.	☐	☑	(1 mark)

STAGE 4: CHECK YOUR WORK

- Have you answered all the questions? ✓

YOUR EXAMPLE

Mr Robert Lee is the manager of a large company in Westerton in the South of England. His secretary is Hilary Wood. She answers the telephone for Mr Lee. She is now speaking to Mrs Carmen Garcia on the telephone.

Hilary Wood:	Good afternoon. This is Robert Lee's secretary speaking.
Carmen Garcia:	Hello, Hilary. It is nice to speak to you again. This is Carmen Garcia from Spain. Can I speak to Robert please?
Hilary Wood:	Hello, Carmen. How are you?
Carmen Garcia:	I have been ill, but I'm much better now.
Hilary Wood:	Good. I'm sorry, Robert is in Scotland today. He is visiting his mother. Can I help you?
Carmen Garcia:	Yes. I'm going to see Robert next week, on Wednesday. We are going to discuss the new factory in Madrid.
Hilary Wood:	I see you have an appointment at 10 o'clock.
Carmen Garcia:	I'm sorry I will be late. I will arrive at Gatwick Airport in London at 10 o'clock and I will travel by train to Westerton. I don't know when I will arrive. I have not got a railway timetable. Have you got a timetable?
Hilary Wood:	Yes I have. If you take the first train after you arrive at Gatwick Airport, I will check the time that this train will arrive in Westerton. Our office is in the tall building next to the railway station.
Carmen Garcia:	Thank you, Hilary. Would you please tell Robert the time I will arrive at your office?
Hilary Wood:	I'll give Robert a message. Goodbye, Carmen. I hope you have a safe journey.

Read these sentences about the conversation. Some are true and some are false. Put a tick (✓) in the TRUE or FALSE box.

STAGE 1: IDENTIFY THE TASK

....

STAGE 2: HOW TO ANSWER

- Have you read the conversation? ☐
- Have you read each sentence carefully? ☐
- Have you checked the conversation again? ☐

STAGE 3: NOW ANSWER THE QUESTIONS

		TRUE	FALSE	
1	Hilary Wood is Robert Lee's secretary.	☐	☐	(1 mark)
2	Carmen Garcia is in Scotland today.	☐	☐	(1 mark)
3	Hilary Wood knows Carmen Garcia.	☐	☐	(1 mark)
4	Carmen Garcia is speaking from Spain.	☐	☐	(1 mark)
5	Hilary Wood is in Scotland.	☐	☐	(1 mark)
6	The telephone conversation is between two women.	☐	☐	(1 mark)
7	Hilary Wood has a railway timetable.	☐	☐	(1 mark)
8	Carmen Garcia will travel by train from Gatwick Airport to Westerton.	☐	☐	(1 mark)
9	The conversation takes place in the morning.	☐	☐	(1 mark)
10	Carmen Garcia is going to give Robert Lee a message.	☐	☐	(1 mark)
11	Hilary Wood is going to tell Mr Lee what time Carmen Garcia will arrive at the office.	☐	☐	(1 mark)

STAGE 4: CHECK YOUR WORK

- Have you answered all the questions? ☐

PRACTICE 1

Elizabeth Dean is a receptionist. She works for a large company in London. Today, many people are visiting the company to see the manager, Philip Elton. A man called Douglas Law has arrived at the reception desk. It is nearly 10 am.

Elizabeth Dean: Good morning sir, can I help you?

Douglas Law: I've come to see Philip Elton. My name is Douglas Law.

Elizabeth Dean: Hello, Mr Law. I'll check my list of Mr Elton's appointments.

(She looks at the appointments' book)

Elizabeth Dean: You are very early. Mr Elton has made an appointment to see you at 4 o'clock today.

Douglas Law: No, I'm meeting Mr Elton at 10 o'clock. I have a letter from him. Would you like to see it?

Elizabeth Dean: Yes please.

(She looks at the letter)

Elizabeth Dean: The letter says your appointment is at 10 am. We have made a mistake. I'm very sorry. Mr Elton is busy now. Can you come back this afternoon?

Douglas Law: No, I'm going to Cambridge this afternoon. Can I come back tomorrow?

Elizabeth Dean: Yes. Please write down when you are free tomorrow and I will ask Mr Elton to telephone you early tomorrow morning to say when he can see you.

Douglas Law: Thank you. I will write down now when I'll be free tomorrow.

(He writes down the times he is free)

Elizabeth Dean: Thank you. I'm sorry about our mistake. I will tell Mr Elton when you are free tomorrow.

Read these sentences about the conversation. Some are true and some are false. Put a tick (✓) in the TRUE or FALSE box.

		TRUE	FALSE	
1	Douglas Law has come to see Philip Elton.	☐	☐	(1 mark)
2	Elizabeth Dean works with Philip Elton.	☐	☐	(1 mark)
3	Elizabeth Dean is the manager.	☐	☐	(1 mark)
4	Philip Elton is very busy today.	☐	☐	(1 mark)
5	Douglas Law has made a mistake.	☐	☐	(1 mark)
6	Philip Elton has a letter from Douglas Law.	☐	☐	(1 mark)
7	Philip Elton checked the appointments' book.	☐	☐	(1 mark)
8	Elizabeth Dean and Douglas Law are speaking on the telephone.	☐	☐	(1 mark)
9	Douglas Law can come back this afternoon.	☐	☐	(1 mark)
10	Philip Elton will telephone Douglas Law tomorrow.	☐	☐	(1 mark)
11	Douglas Law will write down when he is free tomorrow.	☐	☐	(1 mark)

PRACTICE 2

Mr Jan Pilip and Ms Greta Hausman work in the Finance Office of a large company, Laslo International. They both play for the company's chess team. Jan is the captain of the team and Greta is the secretary of the chess club. The chess team plays on Wednesday evenings. Jan has answered the telephone. This is his conversation.

Jan: Hello, this is Laslo International Finance Office, Jan Pilip speaking.

Charles: Good morning, Jan. This is Charles Hansen from Jordan Chemicals. We have met before.

Jan: Yes, I remember you very well. You play for Jordan Chemicals' chess team. You played very well when our team played your team last year, and your team won.

Charles: I was very lucky. In fact I would like to talk to the secretary of your chess club.

Jan: Our secretary is my colleague, Greta Hausman, but she is away on holiday. Can I help you? I am captain of the team.

Charles: Well, the Jordan Chemicals' team should play your team at your office on 13 March. On this day the Prime Minister is going to visit our company so we cannot visit you. I hope we can play your team later in the year.

Jan: Of course. Please tell me when your team is not playing and I will see when we are free.

Charles: I will send a fax to you today.

Jan: Good. I will look at our team's list of chess matches and I'll email our secretary. She can tell you the new date for the chess match. I will ask her to contact you as soon as possible.

Charles: Thanks, Jan. I look forward to seeing you.

Jan: Thank you, Charles. I hope we can win the next chess match!

Read these sentences about the conversation. Some are true and some are false. Put a tick (✓) in the TRUE or FALSE box.

		TRUE	FALSE	
1	Jan and Greta work for the same company.	☐	☐	(1 mark)
2	Jan says "Hello" to Charles.	☐	☐	(1 mark)
3	Jan does not remember Charles.	☐	☐	(1 mark)
4	Greta Hausman is the secretary of Laslo International chess club.	☐	☐	(1 mark)
5	Jan is going to receive a fax.	☐	☐	(1 mark)
6	Charles and Jan have not met before.	☐	☐	(1 mark)
7	The Prime Minister is going to visit Laslo International.	☐	☐	(1 mark)
8	Jordan Chemicals' chess team won the last chess match with Laslo International.	☐	☐	(1 mark)
9	The two men are talking on the telephone.	☐	☐	(1 mark)
10	Charles says "Goodbye" to Jan.	☐	☐	(1 mark)
11	Greta Hausman is going to visit the Prime Minister.	☐	☐	(1 mark)

PRACTICE 3

Ute Böhm works at the Gardens Hotel. She is a receptionist and she books rooms for people who want to stay at the hotel. She is now speaking on the telephone to a man called Bruno Scalini.

It is 10 o'clock in the morning on Monday 8 April.

Ute: Good afternoon – Oh! Sorry, I mean good morning. This is the Gardens Hotel, Ute Böhm speaking. How can I help you?

Bruno: I would like to book a room for tonight and tomorrow night, please. Do you have a room available?

Ute: We are not busy at the moment, sir. Is it a room for one person?

Bruno: No, I would like to book a family room, if that is possible. It is for myself, my wife and our two children.

Ute: We have some very good family rooms.

Bruno: Good. But are your family rooms "Non-Smoking"? Our doctor says my son must not sleep in a room used by people who smoke.

Ute: Yes, most of our family rooms are non-smoking. Is there anything else that you would like?

Bruno: I hear that some of your rooms have a view of the gardens. Could we have one of these?

Ute: I will try to book one. The gardens are lovely at the moment.

Bruno: Very good. There is just one more thing. We are going to arrive at the hotel very late tonight. It will be 11 o'clock. Is this all right?

Ute: Of course. I will not be here but I will leave a message for our Deputy Manager, Paulina Scadeng. She will be working here tonight. What is your name, please?

Bruno: I am Bruno Scalini. My wife is Sophia Scalini; my children are my son, Marco, who is 11 years old and my daughter, Petra, who is 4.

Ute: Right. I will check which room is available for your family and tell the Deputy Manager that you are going to arrive late. I hope you enjoy your stay with us.

Bruno: I am sure we will. Goodbye.

Read these sentences about the conversation. Some are true and some are false. Put a tick (✓) in the TRUE or FALSE box.

		TRUE	FALSE	
1	Bruno Scalini works at the hotel.	☐	☐	(1 mark)
2	Ute made a mistake when she answered the telephone.	☐	☐	(1 mark)
3	The hotel is busy at the moment.	☐	☐	(1 mark)
4	Bruno wants a family room for one night.	☐	☐	(1 mark)
5	Bruno and his wife have two children, a boy and a girl.	☐	☐	(1 mark)
6	The Deputy Manager is a woman.	☐	☐	(1 mark)
7	Bruno's wife is called Petra Scalini.	☐	☐	(1 mark)
8	All the family rooms are non-smoking.	☐	☐	(1 mark)
9	Bruno would like a room with a view of the gardens.	☐	☐	(1 mark)
10	Ute will meet Bruno when he arrives at the hotel.	☐	☐	(1 mark)
11	Bruno's daughter is younger than his son.	☐	☐	(1 mark)

PRACTICE 4

Mrs Roswitha Glana is Head of Department in a large business, RAR Products. She is not in her office today but her assistant, Mr Joshua Silenje, is in the office. He is speaking on the telephone to a woman called Miss Marina Chiesa.

Joshua: Hello, this is Joshua Silenje speaking.

Marina: Good afternoon. This is Marina Chiesa from First Central Bank. Could I speak to Roswitha Glana, please?

Joshua: Mrs Glana is not in today. Can I help you?

Marina: I need to speak to Mrs Glana. It is very important. When will she be at work?

Joshua: She will not be here until next Monday. She is visiting Head Office.

Marina: I must discuss the bank loan with her before the end of next week.

Joshua: I have her diary. I can make an appointment.

Marina: Good. I am free any day next week, except Wednesday. And on Friday afternoon I am going to the dentist. I will visit Mrs Glana in her office.

Joshua: Very well. Oh dear. I can't find her diary. Can I ring you back?

Marina: I'm going out now, I'm afraid.

Joshua: When I find the diary, I will make an appointment for you to see Roswitha. I will ask her to confirm this and she can speak to you on Monday. She will tell you the day and time she can see you.

Marina: That's fine. My telephone number is 077 918442. If I am not there, she can leave a message with my secretary.

Joshua: Thank you. Goodbye.

Read these sentences about the conversation. Some are true and some are false. Put a tick (✓) in the TRUE or FALSE box.

		TRUE	FALSE	
1	Joshua Silenje answered the telephone.	☐	☐	(1 mark)
2	Marina Chiesa works for First Central Bank.	☐	☐	(1 mark)
3	Marina is not free next Wednesday.	☐	☐	(1 mark)
4	Joshua is Roswitha's assistant.	☐	☐	(1 mark)
5	Joshua works for a bank.	☐	☐	(1 mark)
6	Roswitha and Marina are women.	☐	☐	(1 mark)
7	Roswitha is going to contact Marina next week.	☐	☐	(1 mark)
8	Joshua could not find Roswitha's diary.	☐	☐	(1 mark)
9	Marina's message is not important.	☐	☐	(1 mark)
10	Joshua and Roswitha work for the same company.	☐	☐	(1 mark)
11	Marina's telephone number is 077 918842.	☐	☐	(1 mark)

PRACTICE 5

Ingrid Bruckner is a receptionist in a large company in England. She is at work today. A man called Stephen Macdonald works for the company. Ingrid and Stephen are now talking in the reception area.

Stephen: Excuse me, good morning, I would like to speak to Mrs Ingrid Bruckner.

Ingrid: I'm Ingrid Bruckner. Can I help you?

Stephen: I hope so. My name is Stephen Macdonald and I work in the Finance Department. My boss tells me that you can speak German.

Ingrid: I'm sorry. I'm afraid I can't. I only know one or two words like "Entschuldigen Sie" and "Auf Wiedersehen".

Stephen: *(laughing)* I know they mean "excuse me" and "goodbye" but I don't know any other German. I hoped you could help me. You have a German name.

Ingrid: "Bruckner" is my husband's name. His family come from Graz in Austria, but I actually come from Scotland.

Stephen: Really? I was born in Scotland – in the city of Glasgow.

Ingrid: I come from Edinburgh.

Stephen: Edinburgh is a very beautiful city. I love to visit its castle. However, this doesn't help me. I have received a letter from a customer in Germany and no-one in our office can speak German.

Ingrid: I have a list of people in the company who understand other languages. It is in the filing cabinet in another room. I can look at the list and see if anyone can understand German.

Stephen: That would be very helpful.

Ingrid: If I can find anyone who can understand German I'll ask them to contact you. I will explain your problem.

Stephen: Thank you very much, Ingrid, my telephone number is 2407. I must go now – I have an appointment. It was nice to meet you. Bye.

Read these sentences about the conversation. Some are true and some are false. Put a tick (✓) in the TRUE or FALSE box.

		TRUE	FALSE	
1	Ingrid and Stephen work for the same company.	☐	☐	(1 mark)
2	Stephen and Ingrid are speaking on the telephone.	☐	☐	(1 mark)
3	Stephen does not understand German.	☐	☐	(1 mark)
4	Stephen's boss believes Ingrid understands German.	☐	☐	(1 mark)
5	Ingrid Bruckner is married.	☐	☐	(1 mark)
6	Someone in the Finance Department understands German.	☐	☐	(1 mark)
7	Ingrid comes from Graz in Austria.	☐	☐	(1 mark)
8	Stephen says that there is a castle in Glasgow.	☐	☐	(1 mark)
9	"Bruckner" is a German name.	☐	☐	(1 mark)
10	Ingrid and Stephen work for a company in Scotland.	☐	☐	(1 mark)
11	Stephen says "Excuse me" twice.	☐	☐	(1 mark)

PRACTICE 6

Maria Kovacs works as a secretary for a large company in the town of Bridgeville. Her manager is Mr Kurt Hausman. It is now ten o'clock in the morning and Maria is on her own in the office. She is speaking on the telephone.

Maria:	Good morning. This is Maria Kovacs speaking.
Kurt:	Hello Maria. It's Kurt. How are you?
Maria:	I am a little better. I am going to the dentist this afternoon.
Kurt:	I'm glad you are feeling better. I must change my plans for today. There is a problem at the company's head office in Queenston. I have to go there for a meeting this evening. I will collect some papers from my office before I go.
Maria:	Are you going to drive to head office?
Kurt:	No. I will go on the train. Of course, my assistant, Karl-Heinz Schmidt, should come with me. I have tried to telephone him but his mobile phone is not working.
Maria:	He is going to be in the office after lunch. I will not be here but I can leave a message for him.
Kurt:	Thank you, Maria. Could you please check the times of trains from Bridgeville to Queenston? I do not have a timetable. We must arrive in Queenston no later than seven o'clock and we will have dinner on the train.
Maria:	Yes. I will do that. I have a timetable in my desk.
Kurt:	Please tell Karl-Heinz that he must come to Queenston and tell him the time of the train. I will then see him when I come into the office.
Maria:	Yes, I will do that.
Kurt:	Thanks. I hope that you enjoy your visit to the dentist!

Read these sentences about the conversation. Some are true and some are false. Put a tick (✓) in the TRUE or FALSE box.

		TRUE	FALSE	
1	Maria Kovacs is speaking to Kurt Hausman on the telephone.	☐	☐	(1 mark)
2	The company's head office is in Bridgeville.	☐	☐	(1 mark)
3	Maria Kovacs has an appointment with the dentist.	☐	☐	(1 mark)
4	Maria, Kurt and Karl-Heinz work for the same company.	☐	☐	(1 mark)
5	Kurt is changing his plans for tomorrow.	☐	☐	(1 mark)
6	Maria is going on the train to Queenston.	☐	☐	(1 mark)
7	Kurt and Karl-Heinz are both men.	☐	☐	(1 mark)
8	Maria does not have a railway timetable.	☐	☐	(1 mark)
9	Kurt Hausman is not going to drive to Queenston.	☐	☐	(1 mark)
10	Karl-Heinz is a secretary.	☐	☐	(1 mark)
11	Kurt and Karl-Heinz are going to have a meal on the train.	☐	☐	(1 mark)

SECTION 4: FULL SENTENCE ANSWERS

STAGE 1: IDENTIFY THE TASK

The questions requiring full sentence answers appear in Section B of the examination and are based on the conversation provided for Section B. You have to read the conversation and write a full sentence answer to each question. There are 8 questions and each question is worth 3 marks. The instruction normally reads "Write a **sentence** to answer each question about the conversation on the line marked Answer."

STAGE 2: HOW TO ANSWER

- Read the conversation.
- Read each question carefully.
- Check the conversation again.

Remember:

- If you can't answer a question, leave it and come back to it later.

STAGE 3: NOW ANSWER THE QUESTIONS

- Write a **sentence** to answer each question on the line marked Answer.

Remember:

- You must write a full sentence.
- "He is a painter" <u>is</u> a full sentence.
- "He's a painter" <u>is</u> a full sentence.
- "A painter" is <u>not</u> a full sentence.

STAGE 4: CHECK YOUR WORK

- Have you answered all the questions?
- Have you written full **sentences**?
- Have you checked your spelling?

COMPLETED EXAMPLE

Sarah Fong Wah works in an office of a large business. A decorating company is painting all of the offices this week. Someone is going to paint Sarah's office tomorrow. She is now speaking on the telephone to a painter.

Sarah: Good afternoon. This is Sarah Fong Wah speaking.

Manfred: Hello Sarah, this is Manfred Schiff, the painter. I am going to paint your room tomorrow.

Sarah: Hello Manfred. Yes, I know you are going to paint my room but I won't be here. I will be on holiday.

Manfred: That doesn't matter. It is easier to paint a room if no-one is in it.

Sarah: Good. What colour are you going to paint my room?

Manfred: You can choose the colour. Do you have a list of our colours?

Sarah: Yes, but I haven't looked at it. I have been too busy. Do you want me to choose the colour now?

Manfred: No. Someone can tell me the colour tomorrow. I will paint the walls one colour and the doors and window frame a different colour or shade, if you wish.

Sarah: Oh yes, please. That will be nice. I will choose two colours before I go home tonight. My boss, Mr Vincenzi, is in the office next to mine. I will tell him the colours I have chosen and he can tell you at nine o'clock tomorrow.

Manfred: Right. You can choose any colour but not light green. I have used all the light green paint.

Sarah: I hope you will cover my desk before you paint the room.

Manfred: Yes, I will cover the furniture. The room will look lovely when you return from your holiday next week.

Write a sentence to answer each question about the conversation on the line marked Answer.

STAGE 1: IDENTIFY THE TASK

Write a sentence to answer each question about the conversation on the line marked Answer.

STAGE 2: HOW TO ANSWER

• Have you read the conversation?	✓
• Have you read each question carefully?	✓
• Have you checked the conversation again?	✓

STAGE 3: NOW ANSWER THE QUESTIONS

1	What is Manfred Schiff's job?	(3 marks)
Answer:	**He is a painter.**	
2	At what time of day does Sarah speak to Manfred?	(3 marks)
Answer:	**She speaks to him in the afternoon.**	
3	Why will Sarah not be in her room tomorrow?	(3 marks)
Answer:	**She will be on holiday.**	
4	Where is Mr Vincenzi's office?	(3 marks)
Answer:	**It is next to Sarah's.**	
5	Who is Mr Vincenzi?	(3 marks)
Answer:	**He is Sarah's boss.**	
6	What will Manfred do before he paints Sarah's room?	(3 marks)
Answer:	**He will cover all the furniture.**	
7	Why can Sarah not choose light green paint?	(3 marks)
Answer:	**Manfred has used all the light green paint.**	
8	When will Sarah return from holiday?	(3 marks)
Answer:	**She will return from holiday next week.**	

STAGE 4: CHECK YOUR WORK

• Have you answered all the questions?	✓
• Have you written full **sentences**?	✓
• Have you checked your spelling?	✓

YOUR EXAMPLE

Marcus Rieder works in a library. It is now two o'clock and Marcus has answered the telephone. He is speaking to someone called Karina Lorenz.

Marcus:	Good afternoon. This is Metroville Library, Marcus Rieder speaking. Can I help you?
Karina:	I hope so. I have lost my watch and I think I left it in the library. I worked in the library this morning. I was sitting at the large desk near the window and I left the library at 11 o'clock. Have you found my watch?
Marcus:	I'm sorry. No-one has given a watch to me. But many people lose things in the library. Every day at five o'clock my boss makes a list of everything that we find.
Karina:	I am upset. It is an expensive watch. My father gave it to me.
Marcus:	Can you describe the watch, please?
Karina:	The watch is gold. It was made by Rath Company of Switzerland. It is a small lady's watch. The strap is black and made of leather.
Marcus:	I will look at the list at five o'clock and ring you.
Karina:	I will not be at home at five o'clock. I am meeting my daughter at her school. I will be home at six o'clock.
Marcus:	I will not be here then. But I will ask my colleague, Clarence Pinto, to ring you at six o'clock.
Karina:	Thank you. My name is Karina Lorenz and my telephone number is 931 – 4778.
Marcus:	I hope we find the watch. Goodbye Ms Lorenz.

Write a sentence to answer each question about the conversation on the line marked Answer.

STAGE 1: IDENTIFY THE TASK

....

STAGE 2: HOW TO ANSWER

- Have you read the conversation? ☐
- Have you read each question carefully? ☐
- Have you checked the conversation again? ☐

STAGE 3: NOW ANSWER THE QUESTIONS

1	What time did Karina leave the library?	(3 marks)
Answer:		
2	Who made Karina's watch?	(3 marks)
Answer:		
3	What colour is the watch strap?	(3 marks)
Answer:		
4	Where in the library was Karina working?	(3 marks)
Answer:		
5	What is the name of the library?	(3 marks)
Answer:		
6	Who is Clarence Pinto?	(3 marks)
Answer:		
7	Why will Karina not be at home at five o'clock?	(3 marks)
Answer:		
8	What size is Karina's watch?	(3 marks)
Answer:		

STAGE 4: CHECK YOUR WORK

- Have you answered all the questions?
- Have you written full **sentences**?
- Have you checked your spelling?

PRACTICE 1

Mrs Joyce Golding works as a secretary at a college. People come to the college to learn to speak foreign languages. A man called Ian Cameron is now speaking to Mrs Golding on the telephone.

Joyce Golding:	Hello. This is Comlon College. Can I help you?
Ian Cameron:	I hope so. I would like to learn to speak French. Do you have French classes?
Joyce Golding:	Yes, of course. You can learn to speak many languages at our college.
Ian Cameron:	Good. I can speak German and Spanish but I'm going to work in France next year. I don't speak very much French and I would like to learn more.
Joyce Golding:	Do you want to come to the class during the daytime or in the evening?
Ian Cameron:	I'll come in the evening. I am at work during the day.
Joyce Golding:	We have French classes every evening, but some of them are full, and we cannot take any more students. I will see which classes are not full and I'll ask our French teacher, Pierre Blanc, to speak to you on the telephone. What is your name please?
Ian Cameron:	My name is Ian Cameron and my telephone number is 699 0847. I cannot go to a class on a Friday evening.
Joyce Golding:	Right, Mr Cameron, I'll ask Pierre to telephone you this evening. He will tell you about the French class.
Ian Cameron:	Thank you very much for your help. Good morning.

Write a sentence to answer each question about the conversation on the line marked Answer.

1 What is Joyce Golding's job? (3 marks)

Answer:

2 Who is Pierre Blanc? (3 marks)

Answer:

3 What time of day is it? (3 marks)

Answer:

4 What languages can Ian Cameron speak? (3 marks)

Answer:

5 Where is Ian Cameron during the day? (3 marks)

Answer:

6 What is Ian Cameron going to do next year? (3 marks)

Answer:

7 What is the name of the college? (3 marks)

Answer:

8 When is Pierre going to telephone Ian Cameron? (3 marks)

Answer:

PRACTICE 2

Maria Slawinsky works as a receptionist in the office of STN Products, an international manufacturing company. She works in the office in Edinburgh, Scotland. The company's head office is in Brussels, Belgium. A man called Graeme Sinclair has just entered the office and is speaking to Maria.

Maria: Good morning, sir.

Graeme: Hello. My name is Graeme Sinclair and I work for Copyco. Can I see Patrick Duffy, please?

Maria: I'm sorry. Mr Duffy does not work here any more. Can I help you?

Graeme: Yes, I hope so. My company makes photocopying machines and I normally tell Patrick when we make a new type of machine. We have just produced a new, small colour photocopier and I'm sure your company will be interested in it.

Maria: There have been some changes at STN. All of our office equipment is now ordered by people in our head office in Brussels.

Graeme: I see. Could you ask your head office to contact me? Our new machine is very good and it is not very expensive.

Maria: I will check who orders office equipment for this office. If you give me your details I'll tell him or her about your company.

Graeme: Thank you. My telephone number is 0131 273 9811. In fact, I will be visiting Brussels in three weeks' time and I can visit your office with one of the new machines.

Maria: I'll ask the person in Brussels to contact you to make an appointment before you visit Belgium.

Graeme: Thank you. You have been very helpful. Good morning.

Write a sentence to answer each question about the conversation on the line marked Answer.

1 What does Graeme Sinclair's company make? (3 marks)

Answer:

2 What is Maria Slawinsky's job? (3 marks)

Answer:

3 In which country is STN Products' head office? (3 marks)

Answer:

4 What is Graeme Sinclair's telephone number? (3 marks)

Answer:

5 When is Graeme Sinclair going to visit Brussels? (3 marks)

Answer:

6 What time of day is it when Maria talks to Graeme? (3 marks)

Answer:

7 Who is going to contact Graeme Sinclair? (3 marks)

Answer:

8 Who says "Good morning"? (3 marks)

Answer:

PRACTICE 3

Beatrice Simbo works for a company called Matchless Furniture. The company makes and sells tables and chairs. She is speaking on the telephone to a customer called Dietmar Müller.

Beatrice:	Good afternoon. Matchless Furniture. This is Beatrice Simbo speaking. Can I help you?
Dietmar:	I'd like to speak to someone about buying some chairs.
Beatrice:	Yes, I work in the Sales Department.
Dietmar:	Good. I would like to buy some leather armchairs, please. Do you have any in stock?
Beatrice:	We do. Do you want our small or large chairs?
Dietmar:	Small chairs, please. I have two and I would like to buy three more. They are very comfortable.
Beatrice:	Yes, we have sold a lot of them. What colour do you want?
Dietmar:	Dark green, please. Could I collect the chairs tomorrow at about 11 o'clock?
Beatrice:	Of course. Have you got a large car?
Dietmar:	I have a van. The chairs will fit into it.
Beatrice:	Please come to our Despatch Department. I will ask Paul Anderson, our Despatch Manager, to have the chairs ready for you. He will also give you the bill.
Dietmar:	I will bring my cheque book tomorrow. By the way, my name is Dietmar Müller.
Beatrice:	Thank you, Mr Müller. The chairs and your bill will be ready for you tomorrow. Goodbye.

Write a sentence to answer each question about the conversation on the line marked Answer.

1 Dietmar Müller is buying some chairs. What are they made of? (3 marks)

Answer:

2 What time of day is it when Dietmar Müller speaks to Beatrice Simbo? (3 marks)

Answer:

3 How many chairs does Dietmar Müller want to buy? (3 marks)

Answer:

4 Which department does Beatrice Simbo work in? (3 marks)

Answer:

5 How will Dietmar Müller pay for the chairs? (3 marks)

Answer:

6 Who is Paul Anderson? (3 marks)

Answer:

7 When will Dietmar Müller collect the chairs? (3 marks)

Answer:

8 What colour are the chairs? (3 marks)

Answer:

PRACTICE 4

Tamara Göllner is a secretary in a large company, KEA International. Her boss is Ms Agnieska Krupinski. Tamara is now in her office speaking on the telephone to a man called Claudio Sanchez.

Tamara:	Good afternoon, this is KEA International, Tamara Göllner speaking.
Mr Sanchez:	Hello, could I speak to Agnieska Krupinski, please?
Tamara:	I'm sorry, she is in a meeting. Who's calling please?
Mr Sanchez:	My name is Claudio Sanchez. I work for the First National Finance Corporation. I have an appointment with Ms Krupinski later today.
Tamara:	I'm sorry, I can't hear you very well – the phone line is not very clear. Could you spell your name, please?
Mr Sanchez:	It's Sanchez, S-A-N-C-H-E-Z. I have an appointment with Ms Krupinski but I am still in my car. I'm 150 kilometres from your company.
Tamara:	Oh dear! Do you have problems with your car? Has it broken down?
Mr Sanchez:	No, it's the traffic. I think there has been an accident ahead. There is a traffic jam.
Tamara:	What time is your appointment?
Mr Sanchez:	I'm not sure exactly. My diary is in my briefcase and I can't reach it at the moment. I know it is later today.
Tamara:	So it seems that you will not be able to see Ms Krupinski later today.
Mr Sanchez:	I'm afraid not, so we'd better cancel this afternoon's appointment. Could you ask Ms Krupinski to ring me, so that I can make another appointment to see her?
Tamara:	Yes, of course. What's your telephone number?
Mr Sanchez:	It's 0207 499 821. That's my office number. I'll be there tomorrow.
Tamara:	Fine. I'll check the time of your appointment and tell her that you won't be there, and I'll ask her to ring you tomorrow.
Mr Sanchez:	Thank you. Oh, the traffic is moving again, so I must go .. goodbye.

Write a sentence to answer each question about the conversation on the line marked Answer.

1 Where is Mr Sanchez? (3 marks)

Answer:

2 What time of day is it when Tamara speaks to Mr Sanchez? (3 marks)

Answer:

3 Why can't Ms Krupinski speak to Mr Sanchez? (3 marks)

Answer:

4 Why is there a traffic jam? (3 marks)

Answer:

5 Where is Mr Sanchez's diary? (3 marks)

Answer:

6 Which company does Mr Sanchez work for? (3 marks)

Answer:

7 When does Mr Sanchez want Ms Krupinski to phone him? (3 marks)

Answer:

8 Why did Mr Sanchez end the phone call? (3 marks)

Answer:

PRACTICE 5

Ms Bettina Ranwez works as a receptionist for Cortico Products, a manufacturing company in the town of Newbridge. A man called Reigo Laitinen has arrived in the reception area. Bettina and Reigo are now talking to each other.

Bettina: Good morning, sir. Can I help you?

Reigo: Hello. My name's Reigo Laitinen. I have an appointment to see Mrs Menchon, the Personnel Manager, at 11 o'clock. I'm a little early but perhaps she could see me now.

Bettina: Mrs Menchon? She's not here, I'm afraid. She left at nine o'clock this morning and she will not return today.

Reigo: I don't understand this. Look, I have a letter from Mrs Menchon. I have an appointment with her at 11 o'clock.

Bettina: (*looking at the letter)* Oh dear. There has been a mistake. Your letter does say that you have an appointment today, but Mrs Menchon is at a conference all day.

Reigo: Well, I need to speak to her quite urgently. I'm a Business Studies teacher at Newbridge College. Mrs Menchon is going to speak to our students next week and we must make the arrangements.

Bettina: I'm very sorry, Mr Laitinen. Perhaps the appointment should have been for tomorrow, when she will be in her office all day apart from a manager's meeting between three and four o'clock.

Reigo: I can come back tomorrow but I am not free all day. I have some appointments.

Bettina: Could you please write down when you are free tomorrow? I'll ask Mrs Menchon to telephone you early tomorrow morning to arrange another appointment.

Reigo: Yes, I'll give you a list. I'll write down my telephone number as well – here you are.

Bettina: Thank you, Mr Laitinen. I'm very sorry about our mistake and I will make sure Mrs Menchon knows what has happened.

Reigo: Don't worry (*laughing*). We can all make mistakes. Goodbye.

Write a sentence to answer each question about the conversation on the line marked Answer.

1 What is Mrs Menchon's job? (3 marks)

Answer:

2 What time of day is it when Bettina speaks to Reigo? (3 marks)

Answer:

3 Where is Mrs Menchon today? (3 marks)

Answer:

4 What time is Reigo's appointment with Mrs Menchon? (3 marks)

Answer:

5 Where does Reigo work? (3 marks)

Answer:

6 When will Mrs Menchon telephone Reigo? (3 marks)

Answer:

7 Where will Mrs Menchon be most of tomorrow? (3 marks)

Answer:

8 What does Reigo write down? (3 marks)

Answer:

PRACTICE 6

Sigrid Frenzel works at a college. She is a secretary. It is now nearly nine o'clock in the morning. Sigrid is speaking on the telephone to a woman called Mrs Joan Jarvis.

Sigrid: Good morning, this is Northville College, Sigrid Frenzel speaking. Can I help you?

Mrs Jarvis: Hello. My name is Joan Jarvis. My son, Thomas Jarvis, is a student at the college. Do you know him?

Sigrid: No, I'm afraid I don't. There are two thousand students at the college. I don't know them all.

Mrs Jarvis: Of course not. But I am ringing to tell you that Thomas will not be in college today.

Sigrid: Oh dear. Is he ill?

Mrs Jarvis: No, he's fine. But he is not in Northville. He spoke to me on his mobile phone late last night. He is a musician; he plays the saxophone and his band was playing in South Bullied last night. The band's bus then broke down so they had to stay in South Bullied. He is going to return to Northville later today.

Sigrid: I see. Well, thank you for telling me this.

Mrs Jarvis: Could you give a message to one of his teachers? Thomas has finished his project but he cannot give the work to his teacher today. He will bring it to the staff room tomorrow at nine o'clock.

Sigrid: What is the name of the teacher?

Mrs Jarvis: I'm sorry I cannot remember the name. Thomas is studying Business Studies and the project is about Marketing.

Sigrid: I have a copy of the timetable for every student. I can check Thomas's timetable for today and I can give a message to the Marketing teacher.

Mrs Jarvis: That is very kind of you. Could you please tell the Marketing teacher that Thomas worked very hard. He has written a very good project, I'm sure. Tell him that he wants to work in Marketing when he finishes his Business Studies course.

Sigrid: That's good. I'll give the message to the teacher. Goodbye, Mrs Jarvis.

Write a sentence to answer each question about the conversation on the line marked Answer.

1 Where is Thomas Jarvis this morning? (3 marks)

Answer:

2 What is Thomas studying? (3 marks)

Answer:

3 How many students are at Northville College? (3 marks)

Answer:

4 What musical instrument does Thomas play? (3 marks)

Answer:

5 Who is Thomas' mother? (3 marks)

Answer:

6 What does Thomas want to do when he finishes his course? (3 marks)

Answer:

7 What is Sigrid's job? (3 marks)

Answer:

8 What time of day does Mrs Jarvis speak to Sigrid? (3 marks)

Answer:

SECTION 5: MESSAGE WRITING

STAGE 1: IDENTIFY THE TASK

The message writing task appears in Section C of the examination and is based on the conversation provided for Section B and further information provided for Section C, eg railway timetable, calendar, price list, diary, etc. You have to read the conversation and use the information to write a message. The message form is provided and is normally a memo, telephone message, fax, or email. The task is worth 30 marks which are allocated as follows:

• correct details (names, dates, times, etc)	6 marks
• correct content of message (facts, actions, etc)	12 marks
• clarity of communication of message	6 marks
• accuracy of grammar, spelling, punctuation	6 marks
	30 marks

STAGE 2: HOW TO ANSWER

- Read the conversation.
- Look at the information.
- Check what details are required on the message form.

Remember:

- Make sure the message details are correct and in the correct place.
  - Who is it to?
  - Who is it from?
  - What is the date?
  - Is a subject required?
    - The subject line tells the reader what the message is about and must be short. A few words or a name are usually enough.

      Examples

      Subject: Mr Singh

      Subject: Meeting on 12 June
- Make sure you give the correct information in your message.
- Make sure your message is clear.

STAGE 3: NOW ANSWER THE QUESTION

- Complete the details.
- Write your message.
- Use full sentences and paragraphs for the message.

STAGE 4: CHECK YOUR WORK

- Are the details correct?
- Have you given the correct information?
- Is the message clear?
- Have you written full sentences?
- Have you checked your spelling, grammar and punctuation?

COMPLETED EXAMPLE

Read the conversation and look at the table of chess matches below.

Mr Jan Pilip and Ms Greta Hausman work in the Finance Office of a large company, Laslo International. They both play for the company's chess team. Jan is the captain of the team and Greta is the secretary of the chess club. The chess team plays on Wednesday evenings. Jan has answered the telephone. This is his conversation.

Jan: Hello, this is Laslo International Finance Office, Jan Pilip speaking.

Charles: Good morning, Jan. This is Charles Hansen from Jordan Chemicals. We have met before.

Jan: Yes, I remember you very well. You play for Jordan Chemicals' chess team. You played very well when our team played your team last year, and your team won.

Charles: I was very lucky. In fact I would like to talk to the secretary of your chess club.

Jan: Our secretary is my colleague, Greta Hausman, but she is away on holiday. Can I help you? I am captain of the team.

Charles: Well, the Jordan Chemicals' team should play your team at your office on 13 March. On this day the Prime Minister is going to visit our company so we cannot visit you. I hope we can play your team later in the year.

Jan: Of course. Please tell me when your team is not playing and I will see when we are free.

Charles: I will send a fax to you today.

Jan: Good. I will look at our team's list of chess matches and I'll email our secretary. She can tell you the new date for the chess match. I will ask her to contact you as soon as possible.

Charles: Thanks, Jan. I look forward to seeing you.

Jan: Thank you, Charles. I hope we can win the next chess match!

Date	Laslo International Chess Matches	Jordan Chemicals' Chess Matches
13 March	v Jordan Chemicals	v Laslo International
20 March	v SDL Systems	v Pathways Chess Club
27 March	Free	v Secker and Klein
3 April	v Kendo Industries	v Stanway Industries
10 April	v Secker and Klein	Free
17 April	Free	Free
24 April	v Stanway Industries	v SDL Systems
1 May	Free	v PDS

Use this information to work out when both the Laslo International and Jordan Chemicals' chess teams are free and can play the chess match. Write the email that Jan Pilip can give to Greta Hausman about the new date of the chess match. Greta will then contact Charles Hansen.

(30 marks)

STAGE 1: IDENTIFY THE TASK

Read the conversation, look at the information and write the message.

STAGE 2: HOW TO ANSWER

• Have you read the conversation?	✓
• Have you looked at the information?	✓
• Have you checked what details are required on the message form?	✓

STAGE 3: NOW ANSWER THE QUESTION

Email

To: Greta Hausman
From: Jan Pilip
Date: Today's date
Subject: Chess Match on 13 March

Charles Hansen from Jordan Chemicals' chess club telephoned this morning. Their team should play our team on 13 March at our office. On this day the Prime Minister is visiting their company so they can't play as planned.

Charles sent me a fax with a list of his team's chess matches in the next few weeks. The only date that both teams are free is 17 April.

Please contact him as soon as possible and inform him that the chess match can take place on 17 April at our office.

STAGE 4: CHECK YOUR WORK

• Are the details correct?	✓
• Have you given the correct information?	✓
• Is the message clear?	✓
• Have you written full sentences?	✓
• Have you checked your spelling, grammar and punctuation?	✓

YOUR EXAMPLE

Read the conversation between Ute Böhm and Bruno Scalini.

Ute Böhm works at the Gardens Hotel. She is a receptionist and she books rooms for people who want to stay at the hotel. She is now speaking on the telephone to a man called Bruno Scalini.

It is 10 o'clock in the morning on Monday 8 April.

Ute: Good afternoon – Oh! Sorry, I mean good morning. This is the Gardens Hotel, Ute Böhm speaking. How can I help you?

Bruno: I would like to book a room for tonight and tomorrow night, please. Do you have a room available?

Ute: We are not busy at the moment, sir. Is it a room for one person?

Bruno: No, I would like to book a family room, if that is possible. It is for myself, my wife and our two children.

Ute: We have some very good family rooms.

Bruno: Good. But are your family rooms "Non-Smoking"? Our doctor says my son must not sleep in a room used by people who smoke.

Ute: Yes, most of our family rooms are non-smoking. Is there anything else that you would like?

Bruno: I hear that some of your rooms have a view of the gardens. Could we have one of these?

Ute: I will try to book one. The gardens are lovely at the moment.

Bruno: Very good. There is just one more thing. We are going to arrive at the hotel very late tonight. It will be 11 o'clock. Is this all right?

Ute: Of course. I will not be here but I will leave a message for our Deputy Manager, Paulina Scadeng. She will be working here tonight. What is your name, please?

Bruno: I am Bruno Scalini. My wife is Sophia Scalini; my children are my son, Marco, who is 11 years old and my daughter, Petra, who is 4.

Ute: Right. I will check which room is available for your family and tell the Deputy Manager that you are going to arrive late. I hope you enjoy your stay with us.

Bruno: I am sure we will. Goodbye.

Ute Böhm is going to leave a message for the Deputy Manager. She will tell her which room she has booked and when the Scalini family will arrive at the hotel. Look at the information below about rooms at the hotel. Choose a room then use the form to give a message to the Deputy Manager.

Room No	Family room	Non-smoking	View of gardens
1	☒	☑	☑
2	☒	☑	☒
3	☒	☒	☒
4	☒	☒	☒
5	☑	☑	☑
6	☑	☑	☒
7	☑	☑	☒
8	☑	☒	☒
9	☑	☒	☑
10	☑	☑	☒

(30 marks)

STAGE 1: IDENTIFY THE TASK

....

STAGE 2: HOW TO ANSWER

- Have you read the conversation?
- Have you looked at the information?
- Have you checked what details are required on the message form?

STAGE 3: NOW ANSWER THE QUESTION

Message Form

To: **Date:**

From:

Subject:

STAGE 4: CHECK YOUR WORK

- Are the details correct?
- Have you given the correct information?
- Is the message clear?
- Have you written full sentences?
- Have you checked your spelling, grammar and punctuation?

PRACTICE 1

Read the conversation between Mr Kelly and Mrs Bellini and then look at the table below.

David Kelly works in a bookshop in London. People from all over the world telephone the shop to buy books. Mr Kelly is now speaking on the telephone to Francesca Bellini. This is what they are saying.

Mr Kelly: Hello, this is David Kelly speaking. Can I help you?

Mrs Bellini: Good afternoon, Mr Kelly. My name is Francesca Bellini and I'm speaking from Verona in Italy. I visited your shop when I was in London in January.

Mr Kelly: It's nice to speak to you, Mrs Bellini. I remember that you bought a lot of books from us.

Mrs Bellini: Yes, I bought some very interesting books about London and Great Britain. I would like to buy some more now, please. Can you take my order over the telephone?

Mr Kelly: Of course. What do you want?

Mrs Bellini: I'm going to visit Great Britain again next month. Do you have a book about the city of Edinburgh?

Mr Kelly: Yes, I have a very good book which will cost £15.

Mrs Bellini: I'm going to visit York, also.

Mr Kelly: I have another very good book about York. That costs £12.

Mrs Bellini: That's excellent. Could you send me these books please? You have my address. I would like to pay in Euros.

Mr Kelly: I'll check the price and I will ask my assistant, James Hardy, to send you a bill in Euros.

Mrs Bellini: Thank you very much. I will enjoy reading the books before I visit Great Britain.

Mr Kelly: Thank you, Mrs Bellini. I hope you enjoy your visit to our country. Goodbye.

Use the table below to work out the cost of the two books in Euros. One book is called "A Guide to Edinburgh" and the other book is called "A Guide to York".

Use the memo pad opposite to write a message from Mr Kelly to James Hardy, his assistant. James Hardy should send the books and a bill in Euros to Mrs Bellini.

Pounds (Sterling)	Euros
10	15.00
11	16.50
12	18.00
13	19.50
14	21.00
15	22.50
16	24.00
17	25.50
18	27.00
19	28.50
20	30.00

(30 marks)

MEMO PAD

To: **Date:**

From:

Subject:

PRACTICE 2

Read the conversation between Chris Norris and Margaret Lodge.

Chris Norris works in an office with two other people. They buy sandwiches every day for lunch from a company which takes sandwiches to the office. Margaret Lodge, who works for the sandwich company, is now speaking on the telephone to Chris Norris.

Chris Norris: Hello, this is Chris Norris. Can I help you?

Margaret Lodge: Good morning Mr Norris. This is Margaret Lodge. How are you today?

Chris Norris: I am very tired. I had to work late yesterday.

Margaret Lodge: It is nearly time for lunch. You can rest and enjoy a sandwich.

Chris Norris: I did not enjoy the sandwich I bought yesterday.

Margaret Lodge: Oh dear. Why didn't you enjoy it?

Chris Norris: It wasn't very nice. The bread was not fresh.

Margaret Lodge: I'm sorry. Our sandwiches are very nice today. What would you like?

Chris Norris: I'd like a cheese sandwich, please.

Margaret Lodge: What do your colleagues want?

Chris Norris: Terry would like a beef sandwich and Joan would like an egg sandwich.

Margaret Lodge: I'll bring them at 12 o'clock.

Chris Norris: Good. I'll pay you for the sandwiches then. I have your price list.

Margaret Lodge: Right. Goodbye, Mr Norris.

Chris Norris has an appointment at 12 o'clock. He has to send a message to Terry Hall, his colleague. Terry will pay Margaret Lodge for the sandwiches.

Look at the price list for the sandwiches. Use this information to write an email that Chris Norris can send to Terry Hall about which sandwiches Margaret will bring and how much money Terry will have to give Margaret.

SANDWICH PRICE LIST

Egg	£1.10p
Egg and tomato	£1.30p
Cheese	£1.20p
Cheese and onion	£1.30p
Salad	£1.50p
Chicken	£1.50p
Ham	£1.20p
Beef	£1.30p
Tuna fish	£1.40p

(30 marks)

Email

To:
From:
Date:
Subject:

PRACTICE 3

Read the conversation and look at the railway timetable below. Use the memo form opposite to write a message that Maria Kovacs could give to Karl-Heinz Schmidt.

Maria Kovacs works as a secretary for a large company in the town of Bridgeville. Her manager is Mr Kurt Hausman. It is now ten o'clock in the morning and Maria is on her own in the office. She is speaking on the telephone.

Maria: Good morning. This is Maria Kovacs speaking.

Kurt: Hello Maria. It's Kurt. How are you?

Maria: I am a little better. I am going to the dentist this afternoon.

Kurt: I'm glad you are feeling better. I must change my plans for today. There is a problem at the company's head office in Queenston. I have to go there for a meeting this evening. I will collect some papers from my office before I go.

Maria: Are you going to drive to head office?

Kurt: No. I will go on the train. Of course, my assistant, Karl-Heinz Schmidt, should come with me. I have tried to telephone him but his mobile phone is not working.

Maria: He is going to be in the office after lunch. I will not be here but I can leave a message for him.

Kurt: Thank you, Maria. Could you please check the times of trains from Bridgeville to Queenston? I do not have a timetable. We must arrive in Queenston no later than seven o'clock and we will have dinner on the train.

Maria: Yes. I will do that. I have a timetable in my desk.

Kurt: Please tell Karl-Heinz that he must come to Queenston and tell him the time of the train. I will then see him when I come into the office.

Maria: Yes, I will do that.

Kurt: Thanks. I hope that you enjoy your visit to the dentist!

Railway timetable

BRIDGEVILLE TO QUEENSTON

Depart Bridgeville	Arrive Stanwick	Arrive Queenston
12.00*	13.00	14.30
13.00	-	15.30
14.00*	15.00	16.30
15.00	-	17.30
16.00*	17.00	18.30
17.00	-	19.30
18.00*	19.00	20.30
19.00	20.00	-

** These trains have a dining compartment*

(30 marks)

MEMORANDUM

To: **Date:**

From:

Subject:

PRACTICE 4

Read the conversation below.

A woman called Diana Johnson has arrived in a reception area and she is speaking to the receptionist. He is called Michael and his manager is called Andrew Scott. Mr Scott is not in the office today.

Woman: Good afternoon, Michael. How are you?

Michael: Hello, Mrs Johnson. I'm very well thank you. How are you?

Woman: I am very well but it's not a good day. It's raining.

Michael: Yes, you must be cold. Would you like a cup of coffee?

Woman: No thank you. My taxi is waiting. Could you give Mr Scott a message?

Michael: Yes, of course. What do you want me to tell him?

Woman: I see Mr Scott every Monday at 2.00pm. I won't be able to see him on the second Monday in May. I'm going on holiday.

Michael: I'll tell Mr Scott.

Woman: On the third Monday in May I'll be late. I have another appointment at two o'clock.

Michael: What time will you see him?

Woman: At four o'clock.

Michael: I'll tell Mr Scott.

Woman: Thank you very much Michael. I must go now. Goodbye.

Now look at the calendar for May below and use this information to write an email that Michael can send to Mr Scott. Tell Mr Scott about Mrs Johnson's visits in May and tell him the dates of the visits which are changing.

Write the email in the space opposite.

MAY

Monday		**3**	**10**	**17**	**24**	**31**
Tuesday		**4**	**11**	**18**	**25**	
Wednesday		**5**	**12**	**19**	**26**	
Thursday		**6**	**13**	**20**	**27**	
Friday		**7**	**14**	**21**	**28**	
Saturday	**1**	**8**	**15**	**22**	**29**	
Sunday	**2**	**9**	**16**	**23**	**30**	

(30 marks)

Email

To:
From:
Date:
Subject:

PRACTICE 5

Read the conversation between Petra Rezková and Julius Mapanje.

Petra Rezková works in the London Office of a large company. Her manager, Julius Mapanje, is not in the office today. It is now late afternoon and Petra is speaking on the telephone. The date is Monday 11 June.

Petra: Good afternoon. This is Petra Rezková speaking. Can I help you?

Julius: Hello Petra, it is Julius speaking.

Petra: Julius! Where are you?

Julius: I'm still in Hong Kong. It's just after midnight here.

Petra: So you will not be at the office here tomorrow?

Julius: No, I hope to get a flight this morning, so I will be in the office on Wednesday. But it is very good news. Cheng's Stores have given our company a very big order. I spent yesterday with Roland Cheng, the owner. That is why I cannot travel to London until later today.

Petra: That is very good news. Your visit has been very successful.

Julius: Yes, and I have enjoyed myself. You know how much I like Chinese food and you can buy some wonderful things that are not expensive in the markets.

Petra: I hope you have bought me a present.

Julius: Yes, I have. I bought a beautiful silk scarf at the Temple Street Market. It is dark green.

Petra: That's very kind of you. I am looking in your diary and I see that you have an appointment to see Kunal Duggal, the accountant, on Tuesday.

Julius: Oh, yes. Please send him a memo. Please tell him that I am sorry I cannot see him. Please check my diary and ask him to see me on Thursday or Friday at a time when I am free. I need to see him for one hour. You can also tell him the good news about the order from Cheng's Stores.

Petra: I'll do that.

Julius: I must go to bed now, Petra. I am very tired.

Petra: Of course. Sleep well, Julius.

Julius: Goodbye, Petra.

Look at Julius Mapanje's diary for Thursday 14 June and Friday 15 June and use the memo form opposite to write a message that Petra Rezková could give to Kunal Duggal.

DIARY		
	Thursday 14 June	**Friday 15 June**
09.00	Interviewing new staff	Meeting Marketing Manager
10.00	Interviewing new staff	
11.00	Interviewing new staff	
12.00	**Lunch**	**Lunch**
13.00	Appointment with dentist	Golf Tournament (all afternoon)
14.00	Managers' Meeting	↓
15.00	Managers' Meeting	↓
16.00	Presentation to Mrs McGregor	↓
17.00	Finish 17.00 today	↓
18.00		↓

(30 marks)

MEMORANDUM

To: **Date:**

From:

Subject:

PRACTICE 6

Read the conversation and look at the information below.

Mrs Joyce Golding works as a secretary at a college. People come to the college to learn to speak foreign languages. A man called Ian Cameron is now speaking to Mrs Golding on the telephone.

Joyce Golding:	Hello. This is Comlon College. Can I help you?
Ian Cameron:	I hope so. I would like to learn to speak French. Do you have French classes?
Joyce Golding:	Yes, of course. You can learn to speak many languages at our college.
Ian Cameron:	Good. I can speak German and Spanish but I'm going to work in France next year. I don't speak very much French and I would like to learn more.
Joyce Golding:	Do you want to come to the class during the daytime or in the evening?
Ian Cameron:	I'll come in the evening. I am at work during the day.
Joyce Golding:	We have French classes every evening, but some of them are full, and we cannot take any more students. I will see which classes are not full and I'll ask our French teacher, Pierre Blanc, to speak to you on the telephone. What is your name please?
Ian Cameron:	My name is Ian Cameron and my telephone number is 699 0847. I cannot go to a class on a Friday evening.
Joyce Golding:	Right, Mr Cameron, I'll ask Pierre to telephone you this evening. He will tell you about the French class.
Ian Cameron:	Thank you very much for your help. Good morning.

Here is a list of the French classes. No more students can go to those shown to be FULL. Look at this information and choose a class for Ian Cameron. Then use the telephone message pad opposite to write a message that Joyce Golding can give to Pierre Blanc. She should ask Pierre Blanc to telephone Ian Cameron with the correct information.

FRENCH CLASSES AT COMLON COLLEGE

Monday evening:	FULL
Tuesday evening:	FULL
Wednesday evening:	
Thursday evening:	FULL
Friday evening:	

(30 marks)

Telephone Message

To: **Date:**

From:

Subject:

REVISION TEST

QUESTION 1

Look at the picture. Put a tick (✓) in the box for the best answer to each question.

1 **What is this room?** (1 mark)
(a) a factory ☐
(b) a restaurant ☐
(c) an office ☐

2 **What time of day is it?** (1 mark)
(a) morning ☐
(b) afternoon ☐
(c) night ☐

3 **What is the weather outside the room?** (1 mark)
(a) it is sunny ☐
(b) it is raining ☐
(c) it is cold ☐

4 **A man is sitting facing the door. What is he wearing?** (1 mark)
(a) a checked shirt ☐
(b) a striped shirt ☐
(c) a black shirt ☐

5 **What can you not see in the picture?** (1 mark)
(a) a filing cabinet ☐
(b) a telephone ☐
(c) a brief case ☐

6 Who is walking? (1 mark)
(a) the man carrying a box ☐
(b) the woman speaking on the telephone ☐
(c) the man writing ☐

7 Who is wet? (1 mark)
(a) the man outside the room ☐
(b) the man coming into the room ☐
(c) the man going out of the room ☐

8 What shape is the clock? (1 mark)
(a) square ☐
(b) rectangular ☐
(c) round ☐

9 A man is carrying a box. Is it in (1 mark)
(a) his left hand? ☐
(b) his right hand? ☐
(c) both hands? ☐

10 What is on the desk nearest the door? (1 mark)
(a) a telephone ☐
(b) a computer ☐
(c) a wastepaper bin ☐

11 What is the woman with long hair doing? (1 mark)
(a) using the fax machine ☐
(b) drinking a coffee ☐
(c) carrying a briefcase ☐

12 How many men are writing? (1 mark)
(a) none ☐
(b) one ☐
(c) three ☐

13 A man is sitting at the desk on the right. Has he (1 mark)
(a) long hair? ☐
(b) short hair? ☐
(c) no hair? ☐

14 What is between the door and the window? (1 mark)
(a) a clock ☐
(b) a filing cabinet ☐
(c) a clock and a filing cabinet ☐

15 One desk has nothing on it. Where is it? (1 mark)
(a) near a window ☐
(b) next to the door ☐
(c) outside the room ☐

QUESTION 2

Look at the picture. Then write short answers to these questions where it says Answer.

1	There are two buildings in the picture. How many people can you see inside the small building?	
Answer:		(2 marks)
2	What time is it in the picture?	
Answer:		(2 marks)
3	Where can you see a woman using a computer?	
Answer:		(2 marks)
4	Where is the dog in the picture?	
Answer:		(2 marks)
5	A man and a woman are standing in front of the small building. What is the man doing?	
Answer:		(2 marks)
6	What can you see flying in the sky?	
Answer:		(2 marks)
7	Which is parked at the side of the road, the car or the van?	
Answer:		(2 marks)
8	In a room of the large building a man is speaking to a woman. What is she doing?	
Answer:		(2 marks)
9	How many windows can you see in the large building?	
Answer:		(2 marks)
10	What time of day is it in the picture?	
Answer:		(2 marks)

QUESTION 3

Mr Robert Clifton is a manager of a business. He is ill today and not at work. Mrs Pauline Heston needs to speak to him. She is calling the business on the telephone and is speaking to Miss Laura Wilson.

Miss Wilson:	Hello. This is Laura Wilson. Can I help you?
Mrs Heston:	Good morning. My name is Pauline Heston. Can I speak to Mr Clifton, please?
Miss Wilson:	I'm sorry, Mr Clifton is not here. He's at home.
Mrs Heston:	When will he be at work? I need to speak to him. It's very important.
Miss Wilson:	He's ill today, but he'll be here tomorrow.
Mrs Heston:	Would you give him a message, please? I'd like to make an appointment to see him. I have something to tell him about the building he wants to buy in Australia.
Miss Wilson:	I can make this appointment. I work with Mr Clifton and I have his diary.
Mrs Heston:	I'd like to see him next week. I am free on Tuesday afternoon, Wednesday morning or Friday morning.
Miss Wilson:	I'll look in his diary and see when he is free.
Mrs Heston:	I'm going out now. Ask Mr Clifton to speak to me tomorrow to say when he can see me.
Miss Wilson:	Of course, I'll speak to Mr Clifton.
Mrs Heston:	Thank you very much for your help.
Miss Wilson:	Goodbye, Mrs Heston.

Read these sentences about the conversation. Some are true and some are false. Put a tick (✓) in the TRUE or FALSE box.

		TRUE	FALSE	
1	Mr Clifton is ill today.	☐	☐	(1 mark)
2	Mrs Heston is speaking to Miss Wilson.	☐	☐	(1 mark)
3	Mr Clifton is not at work today.	☐	☐	(1 mark)
4	Mrs Heston has Mr Clifton's diary.	☐	☐	(1 mark)
5	Miss Wilson's first name is Pauline.	☐	☐	(1 mark)
6	Mr Clifton will speak to Mrs Heston tomorrow.	☐	☐	(1 mark)
7	Miss Wilson is a colleague of Mr Clifton.	☐	☐	(1 mark)
8	Mrs Heston wants to buy a building in Australia.	☐	☐	(1 mark)
9	Miss Wilson wants to see Mr Clifton next week.	☐	☐	(1 mark)
10	Mrs Heston's message is very important.	☐	☐	(1 mark)
11	Mrs Heston is free on Tuesday morning next week.	☐	☐	(1 mark)

QUESTION 4

Read the conversation and look at the table of chess matches below.

Mr Jan Pilip and Ms Greta Hausman work in the Finance Office of a large company, Laslo International. They both play for the company's chess team. Jan is the captain of the team and Greta is the secretary of the chess club. The chess team plays on Wednesday evenings. Jan has answered the telephone. This is his conversation.

Jan: Hello, this is Laslo International Finance Office, Jan Pilip speaking.

Charles: Good morning, Jan. This is Charles Hansen from Jordan Chemicals. We have met before.

Jan: Yes, I remember you very well. You play for Jordan Chemicals' chess team. You played very well when our team played your team last year, and your team won.

Charles: I was very lucky. In fact I would like to talk to the secretary of your chess club.

Jan: Our secretary is my colleague, Greta Hausman, but she is away on holiday. Can I help you? I am captain of the team.

Charles: Well, the Jordan Chemicals' team should play your team at your office on 13 March. On this day the Prime Minister is going to visit our company so we cannot visit you. I hope we can play your team later in the year.

Jan: Of course. Please tell me when your team is not playing and I will see when we are free.

Charles: I will send a fax to you today.

Jan: Good. I will look at our team's list of chess matches and I'll email our secretary. She can tell you the new date for the chess match. I will ask her to contact you as soon as possible.

Charles: Thanks, Jan. I look forward to seeing you.

Jan: Thank you, Charles. I hope we can win the next chess match!

Date	Laslo International Chess Matches	Jordan Chemicals' Chess Matches
13 March	v Jordan Chemicals	v Laslo International
20 March	v SDL Systems	v Pathways Chess Club
27 March	Free	v Secker and Klein
3 April	v Kendo Industries	v Stanway Industries
10 April	v Secker and Klein	Free
17 April	Free	Free
24 April	v Stanway Industries	v SDL Systems
1 May	Free	v PDS

Use this information to work out when both the Laslo International and Jordan Chemicals' chess teams are free and can play the chess match. Write the email that Jan Pilip can give to Greta Hausman about the new date of the chess match. Greta will then contact Charles Hansen.

(30 marks)

Email

To:
From:
Date:
Subject:

QUESTION 5

Sarah Fong Wah works in an office of a large business. A decorating company is painting all of the offices this week. Someone is going to paint Sarah's office tomorrow. She is now speaking on the telephone to a painter.

Sarah: Good afternoon. This is Sarah Fong Wah speaking.

Manfred: Hello Sarah, this is Manfred Schiff, the painter. I am going to paint your room tomorrow.

Sarah: Hello Manfred. Yes, I know you are going to paint my room but I won't be here. I will be on holiday.

Manfred: That doesn't matter. It is easier to paint a room if no-one is in it.

Sarah: Good. What colour are you going to paint my room?

Manfred: You can choose the colour. Do you have a list of our colours?

Sarah: Yes, but I haven't looked at it. I have been too busy. Do you want me to choose the colour now?

Manfred: No. Someone can tell me the colour tomorrow. I will paint the walls one colour and the doors and window frame a different colour or shade, if you wish.

Sarah: Oh yes, please. That will be nice. I will choose two colours before I go home tonight. My boss, Mr Vincenzi, is in the office next to mine. I will tell him the colours I have chosen and he can tell you at nine o'clock tomorrow.

Manfred: Right. You can choose any colour but not light green. I have used all the light green paint.

Sarah: I hope you will cover my desk before you paint the room.

Manfred: Yes, I will cover the furniture. The room will look lovely when you return from your holiday next week.

Write a sentence to answer each question about the conversation on the line marked Answer.

1 What is Manfred Schiff's job? (3 marks)

Answer:

2 At what time of day does Sarah speak to Manfred? (3 marks)

Answer:

3 Why will Sarah not be in her room tomorrow? (3 marks)

Answer:

4 Where is Mr Vincenzi's office? (3 marks)

Answer:

5 Who is Mr Vincenzi? (3 marks)

Answer:

6 What will Manfred do before he paints Sarah's room? (3 marks)

Answer:

7 Why can Sarah not choose light green paint? (3 marks)

Answer:

8 When will Sarah return from holiday? (3 marks)

Answer:

FURTHER PRACTICE

QUESTION	TASK
1	FULL SENTENCE ANSWERS
2	SHORT ANSWERS
3	TRUE/FALSE
4	MESSAGE WRITING
5	MULTIPLE CHOICE
6	SHORT ANSWERS
7	FULL SENTENCE ANSWERS
8	MESSAGE WRITING
9	MULTIPLE CHOICE
10	TRUE/FALSE

QUESTION 1 (FULL SENTENCE ANSWERS)

Mrs Roswitha Glana is the Head of a Department in a large business, RAR Products. She is not in her office today but her assistant, Mr Joshua Silenje, is in the office. He is speaking on the telephone to a woman called Miss Marina Chiesa.

Joshua: Hello, this is Joshua Silenje speaking.

Marina: Good afternoon. This is Marina Chiesa from First Central Bank. Could I speak to Roswitha Glana, please?

Joshua: Mrs Glana is not in today. Can I help you?

Marina: I need to speak to Mrs Glana. It is very important. When will she be at work?

Joshua: She will not be here until next Monday. She is visiting Head Office.

Marina: I must discuss the bank loan with her before the end of next week.

Joshua: I have her diary. I can make an appointment.

Marina: Good. I am free any day next week, except Wednesday. And on Friday afternoon I am going to the dentist. I will visit Mrs Glana in her office.

Joshua: Very well. Oh dear. I can't find her diary. Can I ring you back?

Marina: I'm going out now, I'm afraid.

Joshua: When I find the diary, I will make an appointment for you to see Roswitha. I will ask her to confirm this and she can speak to you on Monday. She will tell you the day and time she can see you.

Marina: That's fine. My telephone number is 077 918442. If I am not there, she can leave a message with my secretary.

Joshua: Thank you. Goodbye.

Write a sentence to answer each question about the conversation on the line marked Answer.

1 How many people are talking on the telephone? (3 marks)

Answer:

2 What does Marina want to discuss with Roswitha? (3 marks)

Answer:

3 What is Roswitha Glana's job? (3 marks)

Answer:

4 What time of day is it? (3 marks)

Answer:

5 Where is Marina going next Friday? (3 marks)

Answer:

6 Where will Marina meet Roswitha? (3 marks)

Answer:

7 Where is Roswitha Glana today? (3 marks)

Answer:

8 What are Joshua's first and last words? (3 marks)

Answer:

QUESTION 2 (SHORT ANSWERS)

Look at the picture. Then write short answers to these questions where it says Answer.

1	How many people are in the picture?	
Answer:		(2 marks)
2	Where is the clock?	
Answer:		(2 marks)
3	A man is at the window on the top floor of the office. What is he doing?	
Answer:		(2 marks)
4	Two women are talking outside. What are they carrying?	
Answer:		(2 marks)
5	What is the weather like?	
Answer:		(2 marks)
6	A man is at the window above the door of the office building. What is he doing?	
Answer:		(2 marks)
7	Is the main door of the office building closed?	
Answer:		(2 marks)
8	A man is at the door of the office building. What is he holding?	
Answer:		(2 marks)
9	Two women are in the window next to the tree. What are they doing?	
Answer:		(2 marks)
10	Are there more women or more men in the office building?	
Answer:		(2 marks)

QUESTION 3 (TRUE/FALSE)

David Kelly works in a bookshop in London. People from all over the world telephone the shop to buy books. Mr Kelly is now speaking on the telephone to Francesca Bellini. This is what they are saying.

Mr Kelly:	Hello, this is David Kelly speaking. Can I help you?
Mrs Bellini:	Good afternoon, Mr Kelly. My name is Francesca Bellini and I'm speaking from Verona in Italy. I visited your shop when I was in London in January.
Mr Kelly:	It's nice to speak to you, Mrs Bellini. I remember that you bought a lot of books from us.
Mrs Bellini:	Yes, I bought some very interesting books about London and Great Britain. I would like to buy some more now, please. Can you take my order over the telephone?
Mr Kelly:	Of course. What do you want?
Mrs Bellini:	I'm going to visit Great Britain again next month. Do you have a book about the city of Edinburgh?
Mr Kelly:	Yes, I have a very good book which will cost £15.
Mrs Bellini:	I'm going to visit York, also.
Mr Kelly:	I have another very good book about York. That costs £12.
Mrs Bellini:	That's excellent. Could you send me these books please? You have my address. I would like to pay in Euros.
Mr Kelly:	I'll check the price and I will ask my assistant, James Hardy, to send you a bill in Euros.
Mrs Bellini:	Thank you very much. I will enjoy reading the books before I visit Great Britain.
Mr Kelly:	Thank you, Mrs Bellini. I hope you enjoy your visit to our country. Goodbye.

Read these sentences. Some are true and some are false. Put a tick (✓) in the TRUE or FALSE box.

		TRUE	FALSE	
1	Mr Kelly works in London.	☐	☐	(1 mark)
2	Mrs Bellini is Mr Kelly's assistant.	☐	☐	(1 mark)
3	Mrs Bellini answered the telephone.	☐	☐	(1 mark)
4	Verona is in Great Britain.	☐	☐	(1 mark)
5	Mrs Bellini is going to visit York next month.	☐	☐	(1 mark)
6	The book about Edinburgh costs £12.	☐	☐	(1 mark)
7	Mrs Bellini wants to read the books before she visits Great Britain.	☐	☐	(1 mark)
8	The bookshop will take orders over the telephone.	☐	☐	(1 mark)
9	Mr Kelly is going to visit Edinburgh.	☐	☐	(1 mark)
10	Mrs Bellini wants to pay for her books in Euros.	☐	☐	(1 mark)
11	Mrs Bellini will visit London next December.	☐	☐	(1 mark)

QUESTION 4 (MESSAGE WRITING)

Read the conversation between Maria and Graeme and then look at the information below about staff in STN Products' head office in Brussels.

Maria Slawinsky works as a receptionist in the office of STN Products, an international manufacturing company. She works in the office in Edinburgh, Scotland. The company's head office is in Brussels, Belgium. A man called Graeme Sinclair has just entered the office and is speaking to Maria.

Maria: Good morning, sir.

Graeme: Hello. My name is Graeme Sinclair and I work for Copyco. Can I see Patrick Duffy, please?

Maria: I'm sorry. Mr Duffy does not work here any more. Can I help you?

Graeme: Yes, I hope so. My company makes photocopying machines and I normally tell Patrick when we make a new type of machine. We have just produced a new, small colour photocopier and I'm sure your company will be interested in it.

Maria: There have been some changes at STN. All of our office equipment is now ordered by people in our head office in Brussels.

Graeme: I see. Could you ask your head office to contact me? Our new machine is very good and it is not very expensive.

Maria: I will check who orders office equipment for this office. If you give me your details I'll tell him or her about your company.

Graeme: Thank you. My telephone number is 0131 273 9811. In fact, I will be visiting Brussels in three weeks' time and I can visit your office with one of the new machines.

Maria: I'll ask the person in Brussels to contact you to make an appointment before you visit Belgium.

Graeme: Thank you. You have been very helpful. Good morning.

Office Equipment

You should contact one of the following people if you want to order large items of office equipment.

Names	**Offices covered**
Mr Wilfried von Rampay	Brussels, Antwerp, Bruges
Mrs Agnes Horvath	Vienna, Salzburg, Villach
Mrs Martine Blanc	London, Manchester, Edinburgh
Mr Patrick Duffy	Dublin, Cork
Mr Carlo Montez	Lisbon, Madrid, Seville

Maria decides to send a fax to the person in Brussels. Use the fax form opposite to write a message that Maria can send to the correct person in Brussels.

(30 marks)

Fax Form
STN Products, Edinburgh Branch
(Fax No 0131 806400)

To: **Date:**

From: **No. of Pages:**

QUESTION 5 (MULTIPLE CHOICE)

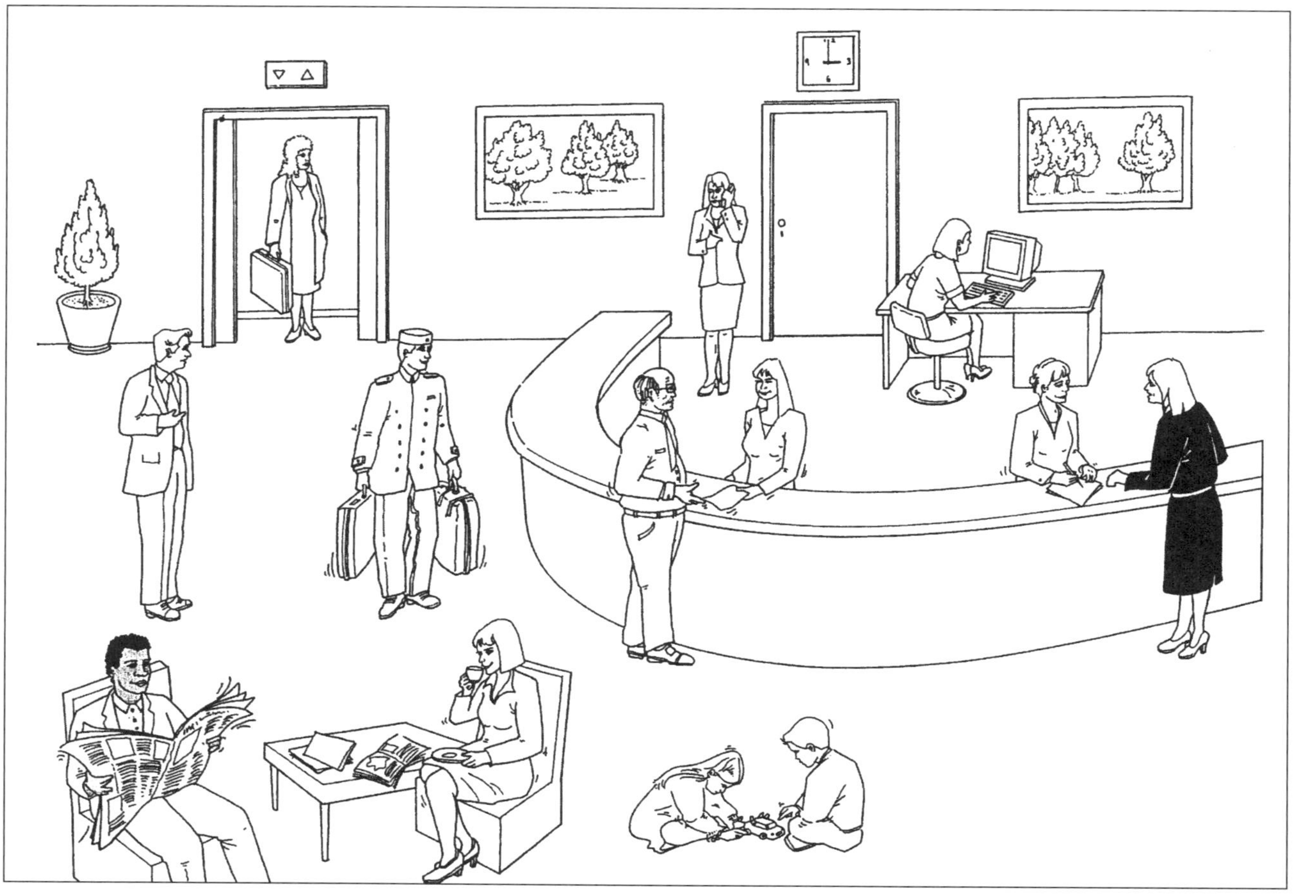

Look at the picture. Put a tick (✓) in the box for the best answer to each question.

1 What is this picture? (1 mark)
(a) a hotel ☐
(b) an office ☐
(c) a factory ☐

2 Is the room (1 mark)
(a) busy? ☐
(b) quiet? ☐
(c) empty? ☐

3 How many windows are in the picture? (1 mark)
(a) five ☐
(b) two ☐
(c) four ☐

4 What is the man wearing a hat doing? (1 mark)
(a) carrying a briefcase ☐
(b) carrying a suitcase ☐
(c) carrying two suitcases ☐

5 How many children are in the picture? (1 mark)
(a) two ☐
(b) six ☐
(c) thirteen ☐

6 What are the children doing? (1 mark)
(a) playing with a ball ☐
(b) playing with a toy car ☐
(c) playing chess ☐

7 What is not in the picture? (1 mark)
(a) a computer ☐
(b) stairs ☐
(c) a telephone ☐

8 What shape is the clock? (1 mark)
(a) round ☐
(b) triangular ☐
(c) square ☐

9 Are the children (1 mark)
(a) a boy and a girl? ☐
(b) two boys? ☐
(c) two girls? ☐

10 A door is below the clock. Is it (1 mark)
(a) open? ☐
(b) closed? ☐
(c) half-open? ☐

11 A man is taking a piece of paper from a woman. What is he wearing? (1 mark)
(a) an overcoat ☐
(b) a jacket ☐
(c) glasses ☐

12 Where is the woman with a case? (1 mark)
(a) near the lift ☐
(b) next to the lift ☐
(c) in the lift ☐

13 What is made of leather? (1 mark)
(a) a suitcase ☐
(b) a window ☐
(c) a table ☐

14 What is on the small table? (1 mark)
(a) a vase of flowers ☐
(b) nothing ☐
(c) magazines ☐

15 What time of day is it in the picture? (1 mark)
(a) afternoon ☐
(b) evening ☐
(c) morning ☐

QUESTION 6 (SHORT ANSWERS)

Look at the picture. Then write short answers to these questions where it says Answer.

1	Are most of the people women?	
Answer:		(2 marks)
2	What is a woman pointing at?	
Answer:		(2 marks)
3	What is the man on the far right holding?	
Answer:		(2 marks)
4	Where is the clock?	
Answer:		(2 marks)
5	What shape is the clock?	
Answer:		(2 marks)
6	A woman is sitting behind the desk on the right of the picture. What is she doing?	
Answer:		(2 marks)
7	Who is wearing a hat?	
Answer:		(2 marks)
8	What is the woman on the left of the picture doing?	
Answer:		(2 marks)
9	What is above the door?	
Answer:		(2 marks)
10	How many people are in the store?	
Answer:		(2 marks)

QUESTION 7 (FULL SENTENCE ANSWERS)

Ingrid Bruckner is a receptionist in a large company in England. She is at work today. A man called Stephen Macdonald works for the company. Ingrid and Stephen are now talking in the reception area.

Stephen: Excuse me, good morning, I would like to speak to Mrs Ingrid Bruckner.

Ingrid: I'm Ingrid Bruckner. Can I help you?

Stephen: I hope so. My name is Stephen Macdonald and I work in the Finance Department. My boss tells me that you can speak German.

Ingrid: I'm sorry. I'm afraid I can't. I only know one or two words like "Entschuldigen Sie" and "Auf Wiedersehen".

Stephen: *(laughing)* I know they mean "excuse me" and "goodbye" but I don't know any other German. I hoped you could help me. You have a German name.

Ingrid: "Bruckner" is my husband's name. His family come from Graz in Austria, but I actually come from Scotland.

Stephen: Really? I was born in Scotland – in the city of Glasgow.

Ingrid: I come from Edinburgh.

Stephen: Edinburgh is a very beautiful city. I love to visit its castle. However, this doesn't help me. I have received a letter from a customer in Germany and no-one in our office can speak German.

Ingrid: I have a list of people in the company who understand other languages. It is in the filing cabinet in another room. I can look at the list and see if anyone can understand German.

Stephen: That would be very helpful.

Ingrid: If I can find anyone who can understand German I'll ask them to contact you. I will explain your problem.

Stephen: Thank you very much, Ingrid; my telephone number is 2407. I must go now – I have an appointment. It was nice to meet you. Bye.

Write a sentence to answer each question about the conversation on the line marked Answer.

1 In which department does Stephen work? (3 marks)

Answer:

2 What time of day is it when Stephen speaks to Ingrid? (3 marks)

Answer:

3 Why does Stephen need to find someone who can speak German? (3 marks)

Answer:

4 In which country was Stephen born? (3 marks)

Answer:

5 Why does Stephen think Ingrid can speak German? (3 marks)

Answer:

6 What will Ingrid do if she finds someone who can understand German? (3 marks)

Answer:

7 Where is the list of names of people who understand various languages? (3 marks)

Answer:

8 Why does Stephen have to leave? (3 marks)

Answer:

QUESTION 8 (MESSAGE WRITING)

Read the conversation between Tamara and Mr Sanchez and look at Ms Krupinski's diary. Use the telephone message form on the next page to write a message that Tamara could give to Ms Krupinski after her meeting with the Chief Accountant. It is now 3.30pm.

Tamara Göllner is a secretary in a large company, KEA International. Her boss is Ms Agnieska Krupinski. Tamara is now in her office speaking on the telephone to a man called Claudio Sanchez.

Tamara:	Good afternoon, this is KEA International, Tamara Göllner speaking.
Mr Sanchez:	Hello, could I speak to Agnieska Krupinski, please?
Tamara:	I'm sorry, she is in a meeting. Who's calling please?
Mr Sanchez:	My name is Claudio Sanchez. I work for the First National Finance Corporation. I have an appointment with Ms Krupinski later today.
Tamara:	I'm sorry, I can't hear you very well – the phone line is not very clear. Could you spell your name, please?
Mr Sanchez:	It's Sanchez, S-A-N-C-H-E-Z. I have an appointment with Ms Krupinski but I am still in my car. I'm 150 kilometres from your company.
Tamara:	Oh dear! Do you have problems with your car? Has it broken down?
Mr Sanchez:	No, it's the traffic. I think there has been an accident ahead. There is a traffic jam.
Tamara:	What time is your appointment?
Mr Sanchez:	I'm not sure exactly. My diary is in my briefcase and I can't reach it at the moment. I know it is later today.
Tamara:	So it seems that you will not be able to see Ms Krupinski later today.
Mr Sanchez:	I'm afraid not, so we'd better cancel this afternoon's appointment. Could you ask Ms Krupinski to ring me, so that I can make another appointment to see her?
Tamara:	Yes, of course. What's your telephone number?
Mr Sanchez:	It's 0207 499 821. That's my office number. I'll be there tomorrow.
Tamara:	Fine. I'll check the time of your appointment and tell her that you won't be there, and I'll ask her to ring you tomorrow.
Mr Sanchez:	Thank you. Oh, the traffic is moving again, so I must go .. goodbye.

Diary for Tuesday 4 March

am		**pm**	
9.00	Free	1.00	Free
10.00	Presentation to Mr Jang	2.00	Write report
11.00	Working on business plan	3.00	Meeting Chief Accountant
12.00	Lunch	4.00	Meeting with Claudio Sanchez

(30 marks)

TELEPHONE MESSAGE FORM

Message To______________________________ **Date**_________________________

Message From ___________________________ **Time** ________________________

Message

QUESTION 9 (MULTIPLE CHOICE)

Look at the picture. Put a tick (✓) in the box for the best answer to each question.

1 What is the picture? (1 mark)
- (a) a street with offices ☐
- (b) a street with houses ☐
- (c) a street with shops ☐

2 How many people are in the street? (1 mark)
- (a) fewer than 10 ☐
- (b) 10 ☐
- (c) more than 10 ☐

3 What is the weather like in the picture? (1 mark)
- (a) sunny ☐
- (b) raining ☐
- (c) cloudy ☐

4 There are two men wearing hats. What are they doing? (1 mark)
- (a) carrying some boxes into a building ☐
- (b) putting some boxes into a van ☐
- (c) waiting for a van to arrive ☐

5 What is between the two buildings? (1 mark)
- (a) a car ☐
- (b) a lamp post ☐
- (c) a tree ☐

6 A woman is outside the door of the small building. What is she carrying? (1 mark)
(a) a shopping bag ☐
(b) a briefcase ☐
(c) a coat ☐

7 Who is talking on the telephone? (1 mark)
(a) a man in the large building ☐
(b) a woman in the small building ☐
(c) no-one is talking on the telephone ☐

8 What shape are the windows in the large building? (1 mark)
(a) round ☐
(b) square ☐
(c) rectangular ☐

9 What is the car mainly made of? (1 mark)
(a) wood ☐
(b) metal ☐
(c) plastic ☐

10 You can see two doors to the buildings. Are they (1 mark)
(a) both open? ☐
(b) one open, one closed? ☐
(c) both closed? ☐

11 You can see some people through the window next to the door of the large building. What are they doing? (1 mark)
(a) holding a meeting ☐
(b) working ☐
(c) eating and drinking ☐

12 A man is at the window above the door of the large building. What is he doing? (1 mark)
(a) using a photocopying machine ☐
(b) using a computer ☐
(c) talking to his secretary ☐

13 Two people are standing outside the large building. Are they (1 mark)
(a) two men? ☐
(b) two women? ☐
(c) a man and a woman? ☐

14 Where is the dog? (1 mark)
(a) in the van ☐
(b) in the street ☐
(c) in the building ☐

15 Are most people in the picture (1 mark)
(a) inside the buildings? ☐
(b) outside the buildings? ☐
(c) beside the buildings? ☐

QUESTION 10 (TRUE/FALSE)

Petra Rezková works in the London Office of a large company. Her manager, Julius Mapanje, is not in the office today. It is now late afternoon and Petra is speaking on the telephone. The date is Monday 11 June.

Petra:	Good afternoon. This is Petra Rezková speaking. Can I help you?
Julius:	Hello Petra, it is Julius speaking.
Petra:	Julius! Where are you?
Julius:	I'm still in Hong Kong. It's just after midnight here.
Petra:	So you will not be at the office here tomorrow?
Julius:	No, I hope to get a flight this morning, so I will be in the office on Wednesday. But it is very good news. Cheng's stores have given our company a very big order. I spent yesterday with Roland Cheng, the owner. That is why I cannot travel to London until later today.
Petra:	That is very good news. Your visit has been very successful.
Julius:	Yes, and I have enjoyed myself. You know how much I like Chinese food and you can buy some wonderful things that are not expensive in the markets.
Petra:	I hope you have bought me a present.
Julius:	Yes, I have. I bought a beautiful silk scarf at the Temple Street Market. It is dark green.
Petra:	That's very kind of you. I am looking in your diary and I see that you have an appointment to see Kunal Duggal, the accountant, on Tuesday.
Julius:	Oh, yes. Please send him a memo. Please tell him that I am sorry I cannot see him. Please check my diary and ask him to see me on Thursday or Friday at a time when I am free. I need to see him for one hour. You can also tell him the good news about the order from Cheng's Stores.
Petra:	I'll do that.
Julius:	I must go to bed now, Petra. I am very tired.
Petra:	Of course. Sleep well, Julius.
Julius:	Goodbye, Petra.

Read these sentences about the conversation. Some are true and some are false. Put a tick (✓) in the TRUE or FALSE box.

		TRUE	FALSE	
1	Petra Rezková and Julius Mapanje work for a company in Hong Kong.	☐	☐	(1 mark)
2	Petra is speaking from an office in London.	☐	☐	(1 mark)
3	Julius will fly from Hong Kong on Tuesday morning.	☐	☐	(1 mark)
4	The owner of Cheng's Stores is Julius Mapanje.	☐	☐	(1 mark)
5	Yesterday was Sunday 10 June.	☐	☐	(1 mark)
6	Julius is not happy about the order from Cheng's Stores.	☐	☐	(1 mark)
7	The Temple Street Market is in London.	☐	☐	(1 mark)
8	Julius does not like Chinese food.	☐	☐	(1 mark)
9	Things in the markets are cheap.	☐	☐	(1 mark)
10	Petra is going to rearrange one of Julius' appointments.	☐	☐	(1 mark)
11	Petra does not have Julius Mapanje's diary.	☐	☐	(1 mark)

ANSWERS

SECTIONS 1 – 5

YOUR EXAMPLE

SECTION 1 (MULTIPLE CHOICE)

STAGE 1: IDENTIFY THE TASK

Put a tick (✓) in the box for the best answer to each question.

STAGE 2: HOW TO ANSWER

- Have you looked at the picture? ✓
- Have you read each question carefully? ✓
- Have you read answers (a), (b) and (c) carefully? ✓
- Have you checked the picture again? ✓

STAGE 3: NOW ANSWER THE QUESTIONS

1 **What is this room?** (1 mark)
(a) a library ☐
(b) a factory ☐
(c) a reception area ☑

2 **How many computers are in the picture?** (1 mark)
(a) none ☐
(b) two ☑
(c) four ☐

3 **Where is the clock?** (1 mark)
(a) above the drinks machine ☑
(b) below the drinks machine ☐
(c) behind the drinks machine ☐

4 **What are the tables made of?** (1 mark)
(a) wood ☑
(b) glass ☐
(c) leather ☐

5 **What is on the filing cabinet?** (1 mark)
(a) files ☐
(b) books ☐
(c) nothing ☑

6 **Are there more women or more men in the picture?** (1 mark)
(a) women ☑
(b) men ☐
(c) the same number ☐

7 **A woman is wearing a flowered dress. Is she** (1 mark)
(a) sitting? ☐
(b) standing? ☑
(c) walking? ☐

8 **Which of these is not in the room?** (1 mark)
(a) a photocopier ☑
(b) a drinks machine ☐
(c) a wastepaper basket ☐

9 **What is between the filing cabinet and the door?** (1 mark)
(a) a window ☑
(b) a drinks machine ☐
(c) a computer ☐

10 Which is the smallest? (1 mark)

(a) a chair ☑
(b) a table ☐
(c) a filing cabinet ☐

11 What time of day is it? (1 mark)

(a) morning ☐
(b) afternoon ☑
(c) evening ☐

12 What shape is the window? (1 mark)

(a) round ☐
(b) square ☐
(c) rectangular ☑

13 What can you see through the window? (1 mark)

(a) an office ☐
(b) a car park ☑
(c) a park ☐

14 Two women are standing and talking. What else are they doing? (1 mark)

(a) eating ☐
(b) smoking ☐
(c) drinking ☑

15 How many people are in the picture? (1 mark)

(a) ten ☐
(b) twelve ☑
(c) thirteen ☐

STAGE 4: CHECK YOUR WORK

- Have you chosen the **best** answer? ✓
- Have you answered all the questions? ✓

PRACTICE 1

1 **What are some people in the picture doing?** (1 mark)
(a) sleeping ☐
(b) waiting ☑
(c) lifting ☐

2 **How many people are in the picture?** (1 mark)
(a) twenty ☐
(b) eleven ☑
(c) none ☐

3 **What time of day is it?** (1 mark)
(a) night ☐
(b) evening ☐
(c) afternoon ☑

4 **A man is coming into the room. What is he holding in his right hand?** (1 mark)
(a) an umbrella ☑
(b) a briefcase ☐
(c) a cup of tea ☐

5 **What is under one of the desks?** (1 mark)
(a) a computer ☐
(b) a clock ☐
(c) a wastepaper bin ☑

6 **Five people are standing together. What is the man in the middle doing?** (1 mark)
(a) reading a newspaper ☑
(b) looking at his watch ☐
(c) talking ☐

7 **Which of these does the room not have?** (1 mark)
(a) stairs ☑
(b) a door ☐
(c) a window ☐

8 **Two women are by desks in the picture. What are they doing?** (1 mark)
(a) writing ☐
(b) sitting ☑
(c) speaking on the telephone ☐

9 **A man and a woman are standing and talking.** (1 mark)
What is the woman carrying?
(a) an umbrella ☐
(b) a clock ☐
(c) a briefcase ☑

10 **What is made of metal in the room?** (1 mark)
(a) the coats ☐
(b) the window ☐
(c) the filing cabinets ☑

11 **What is on the desk on the left of the coat stand?** (1 mark)
(a) a computer ☐
(b) a telephone ☐
(c) a lamp ☑

12 **A woman is speaking on the telephone.** (1 mark)
What is the man on her right doing?
(a) reading a newspaper ☑
(b) coming into the room ☐
(c) looking out of the window ☐

13 **Who is wearing a hat?** (1 mark)
(a) a man in front of the door ☐
(b) a woman outside the window ☐
(c) a woman near the door ☑

14 **Are most of the people in the picture** (1 mark)
(a) standing? ☑
(b) sitting? ☐
(c) walking? ☐

15 **What do we call the five people standing together?** (1 mark)
(a) a queue ☑
(b) a crowd ☐
(c) an audience ☐

PRACTICE 2

1 How many people are in the picture? (1 mark)
(a) eight ☑
(b) nine ☐
(c) eleven ☐

2 What is above the bookshelves? (1 mark)
(a) a television ☐
(b) a table ☐
(c) a clock ☑

3 What is on the filing cabinet? (1 mark)
(a) a vase of flowers ☐
(b) files ☐
(c) nothing ☑

4 A man is standing next to the television. What is he doing? (1 mark)
(a) pointing at the television ☑
(b) speaking on the telephone ☐
(c) writing a report ☐

5 A man is coming into the room. What is he carrying? (1 mark)
(a) a book ☐
(b) an umbrella ☑
(c) a briefcase ☐

6 What time is it? (1 mark)
(a) one o'clock ☐
(b) two o'clock ☐
(c) three o'clock ☑

7 How many chairs are empty? (1 mark)
(a) none ☐
(b) one ☑
(c) six ☐

8 A woman is writing. What is the man next to her doing? (1 mark)
(a) drinking a glass of water ☑
(b) speaking on the telephone ☐
(c) going out of the room ☐

9 Where is the small table? (1 mark)
(a) outside the door ☐
(b) underneath the window ☑
(c) near the shelves ☐

10 Who is looking at a watch? (1 mark)
(a) the woman standing in the room ☐
(b) the man sitting at a table ☐
(c) the woman sitting at a table ☑

11 How many windows are in the room? (1 mark)
(a) one ☑
(b) two ☐
(c) three ☐

12 What are most of the people doing? (1 mark)
(a) standing ☐
(b) sitting ☑
(c) walking ☐

13 Who is wearing a hat? (1 mark)
(a) the man coming into the room ☑
(b) the man standing next to the TV ☐
(c) the woman sitting at a table ☐

14 Where is the television in the picture? (1 mark)
(a) on the right ☑
(b) on the left ☐
(c) in the middle ☐

15 Describe the weather outside the room. (1 mark)
(a) It is hot. ☐
(b) It is cold. ☐
(c) It is raining. ☑

PRACTICE 3

1	**How many people are in the picture?**			(1 mark)
	(a)	three	☐	
	(b)	eleven	☑	
	(c)	twenty	☐	
2	**What time is it?**			(1 mark)
	(a)	twelve o'clock	☐	
	(b)	ten o'clock	☑	
	(c)	one o'clock	☐	
3	**A man is on a ladder. What is he doing?**			(1 mark)
	(a)	talking on the telephone	☐	
	(b)	painting the wall	☐	
	(c)	cleaning the clock	☑	
4	**What is broken?**			(1 mark)
	(a)	the drinks machine	☑	
	(b)	the computer	☐	
	(c)	the telephone	☐	
5	**What is this room?**			(1 mark)
	(a)	a reception area	☑	
	(b)	a bedroom	☐	
	(c)	a factory	☐	
6	**What is the door made of?**			(1 mark)
	(a)	paper	☐	
	(b)	wood and glass	☑	
	(c)	metal	☐	
7	**What is not in the picture?**			(1 mark)
	(a)	a computer	☐	
	(b)	a telephone	☐	
	(c)	a filing cabinet	☑	
8	**What shape is the clock?**			(1 mark)
	(a)	triangular	☐	
	(b)	round	☑	
	(c)	square	☐	
9	**Two people are working at the back of the room. What is the area where they work in called?**			(1 mark)
	(a)	a store	☑	
	(b)	a factory	☐	
	(c)	a theatre	☐	
10	**A man has just received a box. What is he saying?**			(1 mark)
	(a)	"Good afternoon."	☐	
	(b)	"Hello."	☐	
	(c)	"Thank you."	☑	
11	**Does the room look**			(1 mark)
	(a)	quiet?	☐	
	(b)	empty?	☐	
	(c)	busy?	☑	
12	**How many chairs do not have people sitting on them?**			(1 mark)
	(a)	one	☑	
	(b)	two	☐	
	(c)	none	☐	
13	**Is the door**			(1 mark)
	(a)	open?	☐	
	(b)	closed?	☑	
	(c)	half-open?	☐	
14	**Where are some books?**			(1 mark)
	(a)	on top of the desk	☐	
	(b)	on a shelf	☑	
	(c)	in a cupboard	☐	
15	**How many women are sitting?**			(1 mark)
	(a)	none	☐	
	(b)	eleven	☐	
	(c)	two	☑	

PRACTICE 4

1 **Is this picture** (1 mark)
(a) an office? ☑
(b) a house? ☐
(c) a factory? ☐

2 **How many people are in the picture?** (1 mark)
(a) none ☐
(b) nine ☐
(c) eleven ☑

3 **How many people are sitting?** (1 mark)
(a) two ☑
(b) five ☐
(c) eleven ☐

4 **A woman is sitting at a desk on the right of the picture. What is she doing?** (1 mark)
(a) giving a paper to a man ☐
(b) giving a paper to a woman ☑
(c) drinking a cup of tea ☐

5 **What is under the window?** (1 mark)
(a) a table ☐
(b) a clock ☐
(c) nothing ☑

6 **A woman is holding a chair. What is it made of?** (1 mark)
(a) paper ☐
(b) glass ☐
(c) wood ☑

7 **How long is the ladder?** (1 mark)
(a) about 1 metre ☐
(b) about 3 metres ☑
(c) about 10 metres ☐

8 **Is the wastepaper bin** (1 mark)
(a) full? ☑
(b) empty? ☐
(c) half-empty? ☐

9 **Who is wearing glasses?** (1 mark)
(a) the woman standing near a desk ☑
(b) the man standing near a ladder ☐
(c) no-one ☐

10 **What is next to the computer on the desk?** (1 mark)
(a) a lamp ☑
(b) a book ☐
(c) a pencil ☐

11 **A man is looking in a drawer in a filing cabinet. Which drawer is he looking in?** (1 mark)
(a) bottom drawer ☐
(b) middle drawer ☐
(c) top drawer ☑

12 **What is between the smaller filing cabinet and the door?** (1 mark)
(a) a large filing cabinet ☐
(b) a window ☐
(c) a telephone ☑

13 **Who is using a pen?** (1 mark)
(a) a man ☐
(b) a woman ☐
(c) no-one ☑

14 **A man is on a ladder. What is he holding?** (1 mark)
(a) a clock ☑
(b) a desk ☐
(c) a chair ☐

15 **Which of these is not in the picture?** (1 mark)
(a) a coat stand ☐
(b) a bed ☑
(c) a clock ☐

PRACTICE 5

1 **How many people are in the room?** (1 mark)
- (a) one ☐
- (b) four ☑
- (c) six ☐

2 **How many people are standing?** (1 mark)
- (a) none ☐
- (b) two ☐
- (c) four ☑

3 **Where is the calendar?** (1 mark)
- (a) above the filing cabinet ☐
- (b) under the filing cabinet ☐
- (c) between the filing cabinet and the window ☑

4 **What is on the filing cabinet?** (1 mark)
- (a) a vase of flowers ☑
- (b) a picture ☐
- (c) a calendar ☐

5 **Who is wearing glasses?** (1 mark)
- (a) the man looking out of the window ☑
- (b) the man pointing at the clock ☐
- (c) the woman wearing a hat ☐

6 **What is outside the window?** (1 mark)
- (a) a tree ☐
- (b) a house ☐
- (c) an office block ☑

7 **What time is it?** (1 mark)
- (a) afternoon ☐
- (b) ten o'clock ☑
- (c) mid-day ☐

8 **How many desks are next to a wall?** (1 mark)
- (a) none ☐
- (b) one ☑
- (c) two ☐

9 **Where is the telephone?** (1 mark)
- (a) on the small desk ☐
- (b) on the large desk ☑
- (c) on the floor ☐

10 **Who is carrying a briefcase?** (1 mark)
- (a) the woman coming into the room ☑
- (b) the man with the glasses ☐
- (c) the man pointing at the clock ☐

11 **How many chairs are in the room?** (1 mark)
- (a) none ☐
- (b) two ☑
- (c) four ☐

12 **What is this room?** (1 mark)
- (a) an office ☑
- (b) a reception area ☐
- (c) a factory ☐

13 **Where is the computer?** (1 mark)
- (a) under the desk ☐
- (b) on the desk ☑
- (c) next to the desk ☐

14 **What is the filing cabinet made of?** (1 mark)
- (a) paper ☐
- (b) glass ☐
- (c) metal ☑

15 **A man is pointing at the clock. Does he look** (1 mark)
- (a) happy? ☐
- (b) angry? ☑
- (c) pleased? ☐

PRACTICE 6

1 What is the picture? (1 mark)
(a) inside an office building ☐
(b) a street outside an office building ☑
(c) outside a factory ☐

2 What time is it in the picture? (1 mark)
(a) twelve o'clock ☐
(b) five o'clock ☑
(c) seven o'clock ☐

3 How many people are inside the office building? (1 mark)
(a) none ☐
(b) seven ☑
(c) sixteen ☐

4 A woman is in the car. What is she doing? (1 mark)
(a) driving the car ☐
(b) talking on the telephone ☐
(c) pointing at the office building ☑

5 A man with a hat is outside. Where is he going? (1 mark)
(a) away from the office building ☑
(b) towards the office building ☐
(c) into the office building ☐

6 Which is tallest? (1 mark)
(a) the office building ☑
(b) the shops ☐
(c) the tree ☐

7 What shape is the clock? (1 mark)
(a) round ☑
(b) square ☐
(c) rectangular ☐

8 What is in the street next to the two women? (1 mark)
(a) a car ☐
(b) a telephone box ☑
(c) a tree ☐

9 How many shops are in the picture? (1 mark)
(a) none ☐
(b) one ☐
(c) two ☑

10 What are the windows made of? (1 mark)
(a) leather ☐
(b) glass ☑
(c) cotton ☐

11 Where is the tree? (1 mark)
(a) between the office building and the shops ☑
(b) inside the office building ☐
(c) next to a door ☐

12 How many floors does the office building have? (1 mark)
(a) one ☐
(b) two ☐
(c) three ☑

13 A woman has come out of a shop. What does this shop sell? (1 mark)
(a) books ☐
(b) furniture ☐
(c) fruit and vegetables ☑

14 Where is a woman using a computer? (1 mark)
(a) inside the office building ☑
(b) near the office building ☐
(c) on top of the office building ☐

15 Is the weather in the picture (1 mark)
(a) sunny? ☐
(b) raining? ☑
(c) cold? ☐

YOUR EXAMPLE

SECTION 2 (SHORT ANSWERS)

STAGE 1: IDENTIFY THE TASK

Write short answers to the questions where it says Answer.

STAGE 2: HOW TO ANSWER

• Have you looked at the picture?	✓
• Have you read the question carefully?	✓
• Have you checked the picture again?	✓

STAGE 3: NOW ANSWER THE QUESTIONS

1	What time is it in the picture?	
Answer:	**three o'clock**	(2 marks)
2	A woman is writing. Which hand is she using?	
Answer:	**right hand**	(2 marks)
3	What is the woman in front of the desk wearing?	
Answer:	**a black dress**	(2 marks)
4	A man is sitting near a small table. What is he doing?	
Answer:	**reading a newspaper**	(2 marks)
5	A woman is also sitting near the small table. What is she doing?	
Answer:	**drinking**	(2 marks)
6	What is outside the windows?	
Answer:	**trees**	(2 marks)
7	A woman is sitting next to a window. What is she doing?	
Answer:	**using a computer**	(2 marks)
8	A woman is speaking on the telephone. Where is she standing?	
Answer:	**left of the door**	(2 marks)
9	How many people are in the picture?	
Answer:	**thirteen**	(2 marks)
10	Where is there a tree in the room?	
Answer:	**left of the lift**	(2 marks)

STAGE 4: CHECK YOUR WORK

• Have you answered all the questions?	✓
• Are your answers **short**?	✓
• Have you checked your spelling?	✓

PRACTICE 1

1	What is between the stairs and the filing cabinets?	
Answer:	**a door**	(2 marks)
2	One woman is sitting at the desk on the left. What is she doing?	
Answer:	**using a computer**	(2 marks)
3	A man wearing glasses is talking to a woman. What is she doing?	
Answer:	**writing**	(2 marks)
4	How many women are sitting on chairs?	
Answer:	**three**	(2 marks)
5	There are two filing cabinets. What is on top of the cabinet on the right?	
Answer:	**a vase of flowers**	(2 marks)
6	What time is it?	
Answer:	**eleven o'clock**	(2 marks)
7	Where is the woman with the briefcase?	
Answer:	**at the top of the stairs**	(2 marks)
8	Are all the men standing?	
Answer:	**yes**	(2 marks)
9	A woman is holding a cup of coffee. In which hand is she holding it?	
Answer:	**right hand**	(2 marks)
10	Is the door open or closed?	
Answer:	**closed**	(2 marks)

PRACTICE 2

1	What is between the shelves and the filing cabinet?	
Answer:	**a door**	(2 marks)
2	A woman is sitting at a desk. What is she using?	
Answer:	**a computer**	(2 marks)
3	How many women are in the picture?	
Answer:	**three**	(2 marks)
4	Is the door closed?	
Answer:	**no**	(2 marks)
5	What time is it?	
Answer:	**eleven o'clock**	(2 marks)
6	A woman is holding a mobile telephone. Is it in her right or left hand?	
Answer:	**right hand**	(2 marks)
7	What is under the desk?	
Answer:	**a wastepaper bin**	(2 marks)
8	Where is the window?	
Answer:	**above the shelves**	(2 marks)
9	A man wearing a hat is giving something to another man. What is it?	
Answer:	**a box**	(2 marks)
10	What is on the desk to the woman's left?	
Answer:	**a cup of tea**	(2 marks)

PRACTICE 3

1	What time is it in the picture?	
Answer:	**ten o'clock**	(2 marks)
2	How many bookcases are in the picture?	
Answer:	**three**	(2 marks)
3	What is the older man doing?	
Answer:	**choosing a book**	(2 marks)
4	Where is the small table?	
Answer:	**behind the older man**	(2 marks)
5	Who is sitting?	
Answer:	**the woman with dark hair**	(2 marks)
6	What is outside the window?	
Answer:	**a bird**	(2 marks)
7	How many people are in the picture?	
Answer:	**five**	(2 marks)
8	Where is the vase of flowers?	
Answer:	**on the filing cabinet**	(2 marks)
9	Who is coming into the room?	
Answer:	**a woman and a child**	(2 marks)
10	Is there a telephone in the picture?	
Answer:	**no**	(2 marks)

PRACTICE 4

1	How many desks are in the picture?	
Answer:	**three**	(2 marks)
2	Where is the clock?	
Answer:	**above the door**	(2 marks)
3	What is outside the window on the right?	
Answer:	**a tree**	(2 marks)
4	A man wearing a hat is in the picture. What is he doing?	
Answer:	**coming into the room**	(2 marks)
5	How many people are sitting on chairs?	
Answer:	**four**	(2 marks)
6	A man is coming down the stairs. What is he carrying?	
Answer:	**a briefcase**	(2 marks)
7	Are there more women or men in the picture?	
Answer:	**women**	(2 marks)
8	A woman is sitting at the middle desk. What is she doing?	
Answer:	**writing**	(2 marks)
9	A young man is sitting next to the stairs. What is he reading?	
Answer:	**a newspaper**	(2 marks)
10	How many people are in the picture?	
Answer:	**eleven**	(2 marks)

PRACTICE 5

1	How many people are in the picture?	
Answer:	**eight**	(2 marks)
2	What time is it in the picture?	
Answer:	**eleven o'clock**	(2 marks)
3	What is the woman doing who is sitting nearest the door?	
Answer:	**speaking on the telephone**	(2 marks)
4	What is between the window and the door?	
Answer:	**a filing cabinet**	(2 marks)
5	What is a woman bringing into the room?	
Answer:	**a tray with drinks**	(2 marks)
6	Who is wearing glasses?	
Answer:	**the woman on the left**	(2 marks)
7	Is the door closed?	
Answer:	**no**	(2 marks)
8	With which hand is the woman writing?	
Answer:	**right hand**	(2 marks)
9	Are there more men or women in the picture?	
Answer:	**women**	(2 marks)
10	How many people are talking?	
Answer:	**two**	(2 marks)

PRACTICE 6

1	Are most people in the picture talking?	
Answer:	**no**	(2 marks)
2	A man is outside the door. What is he doing?	
Answer:	**speaking on the telephone**	(2 marks)
3	Is the door closed?	
Answer:	**no**	(2 marks)
4	What shape is the window?	
Answer:	**square**	(2 marks)
5	Two women and a man are sitting at a large table. Who is in the middle?	
Answer:	**the man**	(2 marks)
6	A woman is sitting at a small desk. What is she doing?	
Answer:	**using a computer**	(2 marks)
7	What is on the small table?	
Answer:	**nothing**	(2 marks)
8	A woman is sitting on the older man's left. What is she doing?	
Answer:	**drinking**	(2 marks)
9	A young man is wearing a jacket. What is he holding?	
Answer:	**a briefcase**	(2 marks)
10	Are there more men or women in the picture?	
Answer:	**women**	(2 marks)

YOUR EXAMPLE

SECTION 3 (TRUE/FALSE)

STAGE 1: IDENTIFY THE TASK

Put a tick (✓) in the TRUE or FALSE box.

STAGE 2: HOW TO ANSWER

- Have you read the conversation? ✓
- Have you read each sentence carefully? ✓
- Have you checked the conversation again? ✓

STAGE 3: NOW ANSWER THE QUESTIONS

		TRUE	FALSE	
1	Hilary Wood is Robert Lee's secretary.	☑	☐	(1 mark)
2	Carmen Garcia is in Scotland today.	☐	☑	(1 mark)
3	Hilary Wood knows Carmen Garcia.	☑	☐	(1 mark)
4	Carmen Garcia is speaking from Spain.	☑	☐	(1 mark)
5	Hilary Wood is in Scotland.	☐	☑	(1 mark)
6	The telephone conversation is between two women.	☑	☐	(1 mark)
7	Hilary Wood has a railway timetable.	☑	☐	(1 mark)
8	Carmen Garcia will travel by train from Gatwick Airport to Westerton.	☑	☐	(1 mark)
9	The conversation takes place in the morning.	☐	☑	(1 mark)
10	Carmen Garcia is going to give Robert Lee a message.	☐	☑	(1 mark)
11	Hilary Wood is going to tell Mr Lee what time Carmen Garcia will arrive at the office.	☑	☐	(1 mark)

STAGE 4: CHECK YOUR WORK

- Have you answered all the questions? ✓

PRACTICE 1

		TRUE	FALSE	
1	Douglas Law has come to see Philip Elton.	☑	☐	(1 mark)
2	Elizabeth Dean works with Philip Elton.	☑	☐	(1 mark)
3	Elizabeth Dean is the manager.	☐	☑	(1 mark)
4	Philip Elton is very busy today.	☑	☐	(1 mark)
5	Douglas Law has made a mistake.	☐	☑	(1 mark)
6	Philip Elton has a letter from Douglas Law.	☐	☑	(1 mark)
7	Philip Elton checked the appointment's book.	☐	☑	(1 mark)
8	Elizabeth Dean and Douglas Law are speaking on the telephone.	☐	☑	(1 mark)
9	Douglas Law can come back this afternoon.	☐	☑	(1 mark)
10	Philip Elton will telephone Douglas Law tomorrow.	☑	☐	(1 mark)
11	Douglas Law will write down when he is free tomorrow.	☑	☐	(1 mark)

PRACTICE 2

		TRUE	FALSE	
1	Jan and Greta work for the same company.	☑	☐	(1 mark)
2	Jan says "Hello" to Charles.	☑	☐	(1 mark)
3	Jan does not remember Charles.	☐	☑	(1 mark)
4	Greta Hausman is the secretary of Laslo International chess club.	☑	☐	(1 mark)
5	Jan is going to receive a fax.	☑	☐	(1 mark)
6	Charles and Jan have not met before.	☐	☑	(1 mark)
7	The Prime Minister is going to visit Laslo International.	☐	☑	(1 mark)
8	Jordan Chemicals' chess team won the last chess match with Laslo International.	☑	☐	(1 mark)
9	The two men are talking on the telephone.	☑	☐	(1 mark)
10	Charles says "Goodbye" to Jan.	☐	☑	(1 mark)
11	Greta Hausman is going to visit the Prime Minister.	☐	☑	(1 mark)

PRACTICE 3

		TRUE	FALSE	
1	Bruno Scalini works at the hotel.	☐	☑	(1 mark)
2	Ute made a mistake when she answered the telephone.	☑	☐	(1 mark)
3	The hotel is busy at the moment.	☐	☑	(1 mark)
4	Bruno wants a family room for one night.	☐	☑	(1 mark)
5	Bruno and his wife have two children, a boy and a girl.	☑	☐	(1 mark)
6	The Deputy Manager is a woman.	☑	☐	(1 mark)
7	Bruno's wife is called Petra Scalini.	☐	☑	(1 mark)
8	All the family rooms are non-smoking.	☐	☑	(1 mark)
9	Bruno would like a room with a view of the gardens.	☑	☐	(1 mark)
10	Ute will meet Bruno when he arrives at the hotel.	☐	☑	(1 mark)
11	Bruno's daughter is younger than his son.	☑	☐	(1 mark)

PRACTICE 4

		TRUE	FALSE	
1	Joshua Silenje answered the telephone.	☑	☐	(1 mark)
2	Marina Chiesa works for First Central Bank.	☑	☐	(1 mark)
3	Marina is not free next Wednesday.	☑	☐	(1 mark)
4	Joshua is Roswitha's assistant.	☑	☐	(1 mark)
5	Joshua works for a bank.	☐	☑	(1 mark)
6	Roswitha and Marina are women.	☑	☐	(1 mark)
7	Roswitha is going to contact Marina next week.	☑	☐	(1 mark)
8	Joshua could not find Roswitha's diary.	☑	☐	(1 mark)
9	Marina's message is not important.	☐	☑	(1 mark)
10	Joshua and Roswitha work for the same company.	☑	☐	(1 mark)
11	Marina's telephone number is 077 918842.	☐	☑	(1 mark)

PRACTICE 5

		TRUE	FALSE	
1	Ingrid and Stephen work for the same company.	☑	☐	(1 mark)
2	Stephen and Ingrid are speaking on the telephone.	☐	☑	(1 mark)
3	Stephen does not understand German.	☑	☐	(1 mark)
4	Stephen's boss believes Ingrid understands German.	☑	☐	(1 mark)
5	Ingrid Bruckner is married.	☑	☐	(1 mark)
6	Someone in the Finance Department understands German.	☐	☑	(1 mark)
7	Ingrid comes from Graz in Austria.	☐	☑	(1 mark)
8	Stephen says that there is a castle in Glasgow.	☐	☑	(1 mark)
9	"Bruckner" is a German name.	☑	☐	(1 mark)
10	Ingrid and Stephen work for a company in Scotland.	☐	☑	(1 mark)
11	Stephen says "Excuse me" twice.	☑	☐	(1 mark)

PRACTICE 6

		TRUE	FALSE	
1	Maria Kovacs is speaking to Kurt Hausman on the telephone.	☑	☐	(1 mark)
2	The company's head office is in Bridgeville.	☐	☑	(1 mark)
3	Maria Kovacs has an appointment with the dentist.	☑	☐	(1 mark)
4	Maria, Kurt and Karl-Heinz work for the same company.	☑	☐	(1 mark)
5	Kurt is changing his plans for tomorrow.	☐	☑	(1 mark)
6	Maria is going on the train to Queenston.	☐	☑	(1 mark)
7	Kurt and Karl-Heinz are both men.	☑	☐	(1 mark)
8	Maria does not have a railway timetable.	☐	☑	(1 mark)
9	Kurt Hausman is not going to drive to Queenston.	☑	☐	(1 mark)
10	Karl-Heinz is a secretary.	☐	☑	(1 mark)
11	Kurt and Karl-Heinz are going to have a meal on the train.	☑	☐	(1 mark)

YOUR EXAMPLE SECTION 4 (FULL SENTENCE ANSWERS)

STAGE 1: IDENTIFY THE TASK

Write a sentence to answer each question about the conversation on the line marked Answer.

STAGE 2: HOW TO ANSWER

• Have you read the conversation?	✓
• Have you read each question carefully?	✓
• Have you checked the conversation again?	✓

STAGE 3: NOW ANSWER THE QUESTIONS

1	What time did Karina leave the library?	(3 marks)
Answer:	**She left the library at eleven o'clock.**	
2	Who made Karina's watch?	(3 marks)
Answer:	**The Rath Company of Switzerland made it.**	
3	What colour is the watch strap?	(3 marks)
Answer:	**It is black.**	
4	Where in the library was Karina working?	(3 marks)
Answer:	**She was working at the large desk near the window.**	
5	What is the name of the library?	(3 marks)
Answer:	**It is called Metroville Library.**	
6	Who is Clarence Pinto?	(3 marks)
Answer:	**He is a colleague of Marcus Rieder.**	
7	Why will Karina not be at home at five o'clock?	(3 marks)
Answer:	**She is meeting her daughter at school then.**	
8	What size is Karina's watch?	(3 marks)
Answer:	**It is small.**	

STAGE 4: CHECK YOUR WORK

• Have you answered all the questions?	✓
• Have you written full **sentences**?	✓
• Have you checked your spelling?	✓

PRACTICE 1

1	What is Joyce Golding's job?	(3 marks)
Answer:	**She is a secretary at Comlon College.**	
2	Who is Pierre Blanc?	(3 marks)
Answer:	**He is the French teacher.**	
3	What time of day is it?	(3 marks)
Answer:	**It is morning.**	
4	What languages can Ian Cameron speak?	(3 marks)
Answer:	**He can speak German and Spanish.**	
5	Where is Ian Cameron during the day?	(3 marks)
Answer:	**He is at work.**	
6	What is Ian Cameron going to do next year?	(3 marks)
Answer:	**He is going to work in France.**	
7	What is the name of the college?	(3 marks)
Answer:	**It is called Comlon College.**	
8	When is Pierre going to telephone Ian Cameron?	(3 marks)
Answer:	**He is going to telephone him this evening.**	

PRACTICE 2

1	What does Graeme Sinclair's company make?	(3 marks)
Answer:	**His company makes photocopying machines.**	
2	What is Maria Slawinsky's job?	(3 marks)
Answer:	**She is a receptionist at STN Products.**	
3	In which country is STN Products' head office?	(3 marks)
Answer:	**It is in Belgium.**	
4	What is Graeme Sinclair's telephone number?	(3 marks)
Answer:	**His telephone number is 0131 273 9811.**	
5	When is Graeme Sinclair going to visit Brussels?	(3 marks)
Answer:	**He is going to visit Brussels in three weeks' time.**	
6	What time of day is it when Maria talks to Graeme?	(3 marks)
Answer:	**It is morning.**	
7	Who is going to contact Graeme Sinclair?	(3 marks)
Answer:	**The person at head office who orders office equipment is going to contact him.**	
8	Who says "Good morning"?	(3 marks)
Answer:	**Graeme and Maria both say "Good morning".**	

PRACTICE 3

1	Dietmar Müller is buying some chairs. What are they made of?	(3 marks)
Answer:	**They are made of leather.**	
2	What time of day is it when Dietmar Müller speaks to Beatrice Simbo?	(3 marks)
Answer:	**He speaks to her in the afternoon.**	
3	How many chairs does Dietmar Müller want to buy?	(3 marks)
Answer:	**He wants to buy three chairs.**	
4	Which department does Beatrice Simbo work in?	(3 marks)
Answer:	**She works in the Sales Department.**	
5	How will Dietmar Müller pay for the chairs?	(3 marks)
Answer:	**He will pay by cheque.**	
6	Who is Paul Anderson?	(3 marks)
Answer:	**He is the Despatch Manager at Matchless Furniture.**	
7	When will Dietmar Müller collect the chairs?	(3 marks)
Answer:	**He will collect them tomorrow at eleven o'clock.**	
8	What colour are the chairs?	(3 marks)
Answer:	**They are dark green.**	

PRACTICE 4

1	Where is Mr Sanchez?	(3 marks)
Answer:	**He is in his car.**	
2	What time of day is it when Tamara speaks to Mr Sanchez?	(3 marks)
Answer:	**She speaks to him in the afternoon.**	
3	Why can't Ms Krupinski speak to Mr Sanchez?	(3 marks)
Answer:	**She can't speak to him because she is in a meeting.**	
4	Why is there a traffic jam?	(3 marks)
Answer:	**Mr Sanchez thinks there has been an accident.**	
5	Where is Mr Sanchez's diary?	(3 marks)
Answer:	**It is in his briefcase.**	
6	Which company does Mr Sanchez work for?	(3 marks)
Answer:	**He works for the First National Finance Corporation.**	
7	When does Mr Sanchez want Ms Krupinski to phone him?	(3 marks)
Answer:	**He wants her to phone him tomorrow.**	
8	Why did Mr Sanchez end the phone call?	(3 marks)
Answer:	**He ended the phone call because the traffic was moving again.**	

PRACTICE 5

1	What is Mrs Menchon's job?	(3 marks)
Answer:	**She is the Personnel Manager at Cortico Products.**	
2	What time of day is it when Bettina speaks to Reigo?	(3 marks)
Answer:	**She speaks to him in the morning.**	
3	Where is Mrs Menchon today?	(3 marks)
Answer:	**She is at a conference.**	
4	What time is Reigo's appointment with Mrs Menchon?	(3 marks)
Answer:	**It is at eleven o'clock.**	
5	Where does Reigo work?	(3 marks)
Answer:	**He works at Newbridge College.**	
6	When will Mrs Menchon telephone Reigo?	(3 marks)
Answer:	**She will telephone him early tomorrow morning.**	
7	Where will Mrs Menchon be most of tomorrow?	(3 marks)
Answer:	**She will be in her office.**	
8	What does Reigo write down?	(3 marks)
Answer:	**He writes down his telephone number and when he is free tomorrow.**	

PRACTICE 6

1	Where is Thomas Jarvis this morning?	(3 marks)
Answer:	**He is in South Bullied.**	
2	What is Thomas studying?	(3 marks)
Answer:	**He is studying Business Studies.**	
3	How many students are at Northville College?	(3 marks)
Answer:	**There are 2000 students at the college.**	
4	What musical instrument does Thomas play?	(3 marks)
Answer:	**He plays the saxophone.**	
5	Who is Thomas' mother?	(3 marks)
Answer:	**Joan Jarvis is his mother.**	
6	What does Thomas want to do when he finishes his course?	(3 marks)
Answer:	**He wants to work in Marketing.**	
7	What is Sigrid's job?	(3 marks)
Answer:	**She is a secretary at Northville College.**	
8	What time of day does Mrs Jarvis speak to Sigrid?	(3 marks)
Answer:	**She speaks to her in the morning.**	

YOUR EXAMPLE

SECTION 5 (MESSAGE WRITING)

STAGE 1: IDENTIFY THE TASK

Read the conversation, look at the information and write the message.

STAGE 2: HOW TO ANSWER

• Have you read the conversation?	✓
• Have you looked at the information?	✓
• Have you checked what details are required on the message form?	✓

STAGE 3: NOW ANSWER THE QUESTION

Message Form

To: Paulina Scadeng **Date:** Today's date

From: Ute Böhm

Subject: Reservation Room 5

Mr Bruno Scalini telephoned this morning. He wanted to book a family room for tonight and tomorrow night. He wanted a non-smoking room with a view of the gardens. The only possibility is Room 5 so I have booked it for him.

His family are Mrs Sophia Scalini, his son Marco who is 11 and his daughter Petra who is 4.

The family will arrive later this evening at about 11 o'clock.

STAGE 4: CHECK YOUR WORK

• Are the details correct?	✓
• Have you given the correct information?	✓
• Is the message clear?	✓
• Have you written full sentences?	✓
• Have you checked your spelling, grammar and punctuation?	✓

PRACTICE 1

MEMO PAD

To: James Hardy **Date:** Today's date

From: David Kelly

Subject: Order – Mrs Bellini, Italy

Mrs Francesca Bellini from Verona in Italy telephoned this afternoon. She ordered two books and wants the bill in Euros.

The books are "A Guide to Edinburgh" which costs €22.50 and "A Guide to York" which costs €18.00. The total is €40.50.

Please send her the books and a bill in Euros. Her address is in the filing cabinet.

PRACTICE 2

Email

To: Terry Hall
From: Chris Norris
Date: Today's date
Subject: Lunchtime Sandwiches

Margaret Lodge from the sandwich company telephoned this morning. I ordered an egg sandwich for Joan, a beef sandwich for you and a cheese sandwich for me. She will bring them at 12 o'clock.

I have an appointment then so please can you give her the money for the sandwiches. The egg sandwich costs £1.10, the beef sandwich costs £1.30 and the cheese sandwich costs £1.20.

The total for Margaret is £3.60.

PRACTICE 3

MEMORANDUM

To: Karl-Heinz Schmidt **Date:** Today's date

From: Maria Kovacs

Subject: Meeting Today at Head Office

Kurt rang this morning while you were not in the office. He tried to call you on your mobile phone but it is not working.

He has a change of plan for today. There is a problem at head office and you and Kurt must go to a meeting there this evening. He will meet you in the office this afternoon when he calls to collect some papers.

The train to Queenston leaves Bridgeville at 16.00 and arrives at 18.30. You can have dinner on the train.

PRACTICE 4

Email

To: Mr Scott
From: Michael
Date: Today's date
Subject: Mrs Johnson

Mrs Diana Johnson visited the office. She normally sees you every Monday at 2.00pm but this will not be possible in May.

On 3, 24 and 31 May she can see you as usual at 2pm but not on 10 and 17 May.

On 10 May she is on holiday so she can't see you at all.

On 17 May she can't see you at 2 o'clock because she has another appointment but she will see you at 4 o'clock.

PRACTICE 5

MEMORANDUM

To: Kunal Duggal **Date:** 11 June

From: Petra Rezková

Subject: Meeting with Julius Mapanje tomorrow

Julius Mapanje telephoned this afternoon. He has an appointment with you tomorrow but he is still in Hong Kong and won't be in the office until Wednesday 13 June.

He is sorry he can't see you as planned but he is free on Friday 15 June at 10 o'clock or 11 o'clock. He needs about one hour with you. Please confirm which is the best time for you.

He also some very good news. Cheng's Stores have given us a very big order.

PRACTICE 6

Telephone Message

To: Pierre Blanc **Date:** Today's date

From: Joyce Golding

Subject: French Classes

Mr Ian Cameron telephoned today. He wants to learn French because he's going to work in France next year. He wants to come to an evening class because he is at work during the day. He cannot come on Friday.

The classes on Monday, Tuesday and Thursday evenings are full. The Wednesday class is not full so he can come to this.

Please telephone him this evening. His number is 699 0847.

ANSWERS

FURTHER PRACTICE

QUESTION	TASK
1	FULL SENTENCE ANSWERS
2	SHORT ANSWERS
3	TRUE/FALSE
4	MESSAGE WRITING
5	MULTIPLE CHOICE
6	SHORT ANSWERS
7	FULL SENTENCE ANSWERS
8	MESSAGE WRITING
9	MULTIPLE CHOICE
10	TRUE/FALSE

QUESTION 1 (FULL SENTENCE ANSWERS)

1	How many people are talking on the telephone?	(3 marks)
Answer:	**Two people are talking on the telephone.**	
2	What does Marina wish to discuss with Roswitha?	(3 marks)
Answer:	**She wishes to discuss the bank loan with her.**	
3	What is Roswitha Glana's job?	(3 marks)
Answer:	**She is the Head of a Department at RAR Products.**	
4	What time of day is it?	(3 marks)
Answer:	**It is afternoon.**	
5	Where is Marina going next Friday?	(3 marks)
Answer:	**She is going to the dentist next Friday.**	
6	Where will Marina meet Roswitha?	(3 marks)
Answer:	**She will meet her in Roswitha's office.**	
7	Where is Roswitha Glana today?	(3 marks)
Answer:	**She is visiting Head Office.**	
8	What are Joshua's first and last words?	(3 marks)
Answer:	**His first and last words are "Hello" and "Goodbye".**	

QUESTION 2 (SHORT ANSWERS)

1	How many people are in the picture?	
Answer:	**sixteen**	(2 marks)
2	Where is the clock?	
Answer:	**on top of the office building**	(2 marks)
3	A man is at the window on the top floor of the office. What is he doing?	
Answer:	**speaking on the telephone**	(2 marks)
4	Two women are talking outside. What are they carrying?	
Answer:	**briefcases**	(2 marks)
5	What is the weather like?	
Answer:	**raining**	(2 marks)
6	A man is at the window above the door of the office building. What is he doing?	
Answer:	**cleaning the window**	(2 marks)
7	Is the main door of the office building closed?	
Answer:	**yes**	(2 marks)
8	A man is at the door of the office building. What is he holding?	
Answer:	**an umbrella**	(2 marks)
9	Two women are in the window next to the tree. What are they doing?	
Answer:	**drinking**	(2 marks)
10	Are there more women or men in the office building?	
Answer:	**women**	(2 marks)

QUESTION 3 (TRUE/FALSE)

		TRUE	FALSE	
1	Mr Kelly works in London.	☑	☐	(1 mark)
2	Mrs Bellini is Mr Kelly's assistant.	☐	☑	(1 mark)
3	Mrs Bellini answered the telephone.	☐	☑	(1 mark)
4	Verona is in Great Britain.	☐	☑	(1 mark)
5	Mrs Bellini is going to visit York next month.	☑	☐	(1 mark)
6	The book about Edinburgh costs £12.	☐	☑	(1 mark)
7	Mrs Bellini wants to read the books before she visits Great Britain.	☑	☐	(1 mark)
8	The bookshop will take orders over the telephone.	☑	☐	(1 mark)
9	Mr Kelly is going to visit Edinburgh.	☐	☑	(1 mark)
10	Mrs Bellini wants to pay for her books in Euros.	☑	☐	(1 mark)
11	Mrs Bellini will visit London next December.	☐	☑	(1 mark)

QUESTION 4 (MESSAGE WRITING)

Fax Form
STN Products, Edinburgh Branch
(Fax No 0131 806400)

To: Mrs Martine Blanc **Date:** Today's date

From: Ms Maria Slawinsky **No. of Pages:** 1

Mr Graeme Sinclair who works for Copyco came to see Patrick Duffy today. I told him that all office equipment is now ordered from our Head Office in Brussels.

Mr Sinclair's company has produced a new, small colour photocopier that is not expensive. He has provided equipment for STN before.

He is visiting Brussels in three weeks' time and he would like to visit you. He can show you the new photocopier then. His telephone number is 0131 273 9811. Please phone him to make an appointment.

QUESTION 5 (MULTIPLE CHOICE)

1 What is this picture? (1 mark)
- (a) a hotel ☑
- (b) an office ☐
- (c) a factory ☐

2 Is the room (1 mark)
- (a) busy? ☑
- (b) quiet? ☐
- (c) empty? ☐

3 How many windows are in the picture? (1 mark)
- (a) five ☐
- (b) two ☑
- (c) four ☐

4 What is the man wearing a hat doing? (1 mark)
- (a) carrying a briefcase ☐
- (b) carrying a suitcase ☐
- (c) carrying two suitcases ☑

5 How many children are in the picture? (1 mark)
- (a) two ☑
- (b) six ☐
- (c) thirteen ☐

6 What are the children doing? (1 mark)
- (a) playing with a ball ☐
- (b) playing with a toy car ☑
- (c) playing chess ☐

7 What is not in the picture? (1 mark)
- (a) a computer ☐
- (b) stairs ☑
- (c) a telephone ☐

8 What shape is the clock? (1 mark)
- (a) round ☐
- (b) triangular ☐
- (c) square ☑

9 Are the children (1 mark)
- (a) a boy and a girl? ☑
- (b) two boys? ☐
- (c) two girls? ☐

10 A door is below the clock. Is it (1 mark)
- (a) open? ☐
- (b) closed? ☑
- (c) half-open? ☐

11 A man is taking a piece of paper from a woman. What is he wearing? (1 mark)
- (a) an overcoat ☐
- (b) a jacket ☐
- (c) glasses ☑

12 Where is the woman with a case? (1 mark)
- (a) near the lift ☐
- (b) next to the lift ☐
- (c) in the lift ☑

13 What is made of leather? (1 mark)

(a)	a suitcase	☑
(b)	a window	☐
(c)	a table	☐

14 What is on the small table? (1 mark)

(a)	a vase of flowers	☐
(b)	nothing	☐
(c)	magazines	☑

15 What time of day is it in the picture? (1 mark)

(a)	afternoon	☑
(b)	evening	☐
(c)	morning	☐

QUESTION 6 (SHORT ANSWERS)

1	Are most of the people women?	
Answer:	**no**	(2 marks)
2	What is a woman pointing at?	
Answer:	**the drinks machine**	(2 marks)
3	What is the man on the far right holding?	
Answer:	**a briefcase**	(2 marks)
4	Where is the clock?	
Answer:	**above the door**	(2 marks)
5	What shape is the clock?	
Answer:	**round**	(2 marks)
6	A woman is sitting behind the desk on the right of the picture. What is she doing?	
Answer:	**speaking on the telephone**	(2 marks)
7	Who is wearing a hat?	
Answer:	**the man on the ladder**	(2 marks)
8	What is the woman on the left of the picture doing?	
Answer:	**using a computer**	(2 marks)
9	What is above the door?	
Answer:	**the clock**	(2 marks)
10	How many people are in the store?	
Answer:	**two**	(2 marks)

QUESTION 7 (FULL SENTENCE ANSWERS)

1 In which department does Stephen work? (3 marks)

Answer: He works in the Finance Department.

2 What time of day is it when Stephen speaks to Ingrid? (3 marks)

Answer: He speaks to her in the morning.

3 Why does Stephen need to find someone who can speak German? (3 marks)

Answer: He has received a letter in German and no-one in his office can speak German.

4 In which country was Stephen born? (3 marks)

Answer: He was born in Scotland.

5 Why does Stephen think Ingrid can speak German? (3 marks)

Answer: He thinks she can speak German because she has a German name.

6 What will Ingrid do if she finds someone who can understand German? (3 marks)

Answer: She will ask them to contact Stephen.

7 Where is the list of names of people who understand various languages? (3 marks)

Answer: It is in the filing cabinet in another room.

8 Why does Stephen have to leave? (3 marks)

Answer: He has to leave because he has an appointment.

QUESTION 8 (MESSAGE WRITING)

TELEPHONE MESSAGE FORM

Message To Agnieska Krupinski **Date** 4 March

Message From Tamara Göllner **Time** 3.30pm

Message

Mr Claudio Sanchez from First National Finance Corporation telephoned. You have a meeting with him at 4.00pm.

He is sorry but he must cancel his appointment with you today because he is in a traffic jam 150 kilometres from here.

Please can you telephone him to make another appointment. His telephone number is 0207 499 821 and he is in his office all day tomorrow.

QUESTION 9 (MULTIPLE CHOICE)

1 **What is the picture?** (1 mark)
(a) a street with offices ☑
(b) a street with houses ☐
(c) a street with shops ☐

2 **How many people are in the street?** (1 mark)
(a) fewer than 10 ☑
(b) 10 ☐
(c) more than 10 ☐

3 **What is the weather like in the picture?** (1 mark)
(a) sunny ☐
(b) raining ☐
(c) cloudy ☑

4 **There are two men wearing hats. What are they doing?** (1 mark)
(a) carrying some boxes into a building ☑
(b) putting some boxes into a van ☐
(c) waiting for a van to arrive ☐

5 **What is between the two buildings?** (1 mark)
(a) a car ☐
(b) a lamp post ☑
(c) a tree ☐

6 **A woman is outside the door of the small building. What is she carrying?** (1 mark)
(a) a shopping bag ☐
(b) a briefcase ☑
(c) a coat ☐

7 **Who is talking on the telephone?** (1 mark)
(a) a man in the large building ☐
(b) a woman in the small building ☐
(c) no-one is talking on the telephone ☑

8 **What shape are the windows in the large building?** (1 mark)
(a) round ☐
(b) square ☐
(c) rectangular ☑

9 **What is the car mainly made of?** (1 mark)
(a) wood ☐
(b) metal ☑
(c) plastic ☐

10 **You can see two doors to the buildings. Are they** (1 mark)
(a) both open? ☐
(b) one open, one closed? ☑
(c) both closed? ☐

11 **You can see some people through the window next to the door of the large building. What are they doing?** (1 mark)
(a) holding a meeting ☐
(b) working ☐
(c) eating and drinking ☑

12 A man is at the window above the door of the large building. What is he doing? (1 mark)
- (a) using a photocopying machine ☑
- (b) using a computer ☐
- (c) talking to his secretary ☐

13 Two people are standing outside the large building. Are they (1 mark)
- (a) two men? ☑
- (b) two women? ☐
- (c) a man and a woman? ☐

14 Where is the dog? (1 mark)
- (a) in the van ☐
- (b) in the street ☑
- (c) in the building ☐

15 Are most people in the picture (1 mark)
- (a) inside the buildings? ☑
- (b) outside the buildings? ☐
- (c) beside the buildings? ☐

QUESTION 10 (TRUE/FALSE)

		TRUE	FALSE	
1	Petra Rezková and Julius Mapanje work for a company in Hong Kong.	☐	☑	(1 mark)
2	Petra is speaking from an office in London.	☑	☐	(1 mark)
3	Julius will fly from Hong Kong on Tuesday morning.	☑	☐	(1 mark)
4	The owner of Cheng's Stores is Julius Mapanje.	☐	☑	(1 mark)
5	Yesterday was Sunday 10 June.	☑	☐	(1 mark)
6	Julius is not happy about the order from Cheng's Stores.	☐	☑	(1 mark)
7	The Temple Street Market is in London.	☐	☑	(1 mark)
8	Julius does not like Chinese food.	☐	☑	(1 mark)
9	Things in the markets are cheap.	☑	☐	(1 mark)
10	Petra is going to rearrange one of Julius' appointments.	☑	☐	(1 mark)
11	Petra does not have Julius Mapanje's diary	☐	☑	(1 mark)

GLOSSARY

a
able
about
above
accident
accountant
accuracy
actions
actually
address
addresses
aeroplane
afraid
after
afternoon
again
agreed
ahead
airport
all
allocated
also
am
amount
an
and
angry
another
answer
answered
answers
any
anyone
anything
apart
appear
appointment
appropriate
April
are
area
armchairs
arrange
arrangements
arrive
arrived
arrives
as
ask
asking
assistant
at
audience
Australia
Austria
available
away
back
bag
ball
band
bank
based
basket
baskets
be
beautiful
because
bed
bedroom
beef
been
before
behind
Belgium
believes
below
beside
best
better
between
big
bigger
bill
bin
bird
black
block
blue
book

bookcases
booked
books
bookshelves
bookshop
born
boss
both
bottom
bought
box
boxes
boy
boys
bread
briefcase
briefcases
bring
bringing
Britain
broke
broken
Brussels
building
buildings
bus
business
Business Studies
busy
but
buy

buying
by
bye
cabinet
cabinets
cake
calendar
call
called
calling
calls
came
can
can't
cancel
cannot
captain
car
car park
carefully
carrying
case
castle
certainly
chair
chairs
change
changes
changing
cheap
check

checked
cheese
cheque
chess
child
children
Chinese
choice
choose
choosing
chosen
cities
city
clarity
class
classes
cleaning
clear
clock
closed
cloudy
club
coat
coat stand
coats
coffee
cold
colleague
colleagues
collect
college

colour
colours
come
comes
comfortable
coming
communication
company
computer
computers
conference
confirm
contact
content
conversation
copy
correct
cost
costs
cotton
could
country
course
cover
crowd
cup
cupboard
cups
customer
dark
date

dates
daughter
day
daytime
dear
December
decide
decides
decorating
delayed
dentist
department
deputy
describe
desk
desks
despatch
details
diary
did
didn't
different
dining
dinner
disappointed
discuss
do
doctor
does
doesn't
dog

doing
don't
door
doors
down
drawer
dress
drink
drinking
drinks
drinks machine
drive
driving
during
each
early
easier
eating
egg
eight
either
electrical
eleven
else
email
empty
end
ended
England
enjoy
enjoyed

entered
entering
equipment
etc
Euros
evening
evenings
every
everything
exactly
examination
excellent
except
excuse
expensive
explain
eyes
facing
fact
facts
factory
false
family
far
father
favourite
fax
feeling
few
fewer
files

filing
filing cabinet
finance
Finance Department
find
finds
fine
finished
finishes
first
fit
five
flat
flight
floor
floors
flowered
flowers
fly
flying
food
follows
for
foreign
form
forward
found
four
frame
France
free

French
fresh
Friday
from
front
fruit
full
furniture
gardens
gave
German
Germany
get
girl
girls
give
given
giving
glad
glass
glasses
go
going
gold
good
goodbye
got
grammar
Great Britain
green
guide

had	holiday	is
hair	home	it
half-empty	Hong Kong	it's
half-open	hope	Italy
hand	hoped	its
hands	hot	jacket
happened	hotel	jam
happy	hour	job
hard	house	journey
has	houses	June
hat	how	just
hats	however	keep
have	husband	kilometres
have to	I	kind
haven't	I'd	know
he	I'll	knows
he'll	I'm	ladder
he's	I've	lady
head	identify	lamp
head office	if	languages
hear	ill	large
hello	important	larger
help	in	last
helped	information	late
helpful	inside	later
her	instruction	laughing
here	instrument	law
hill	interested	learn
him	interesting	leather
his	international	leave
holding	into	leaves

left
letter
library
lift
lifting
light
like
line
list
listen
little
live
loan
London
long
look
look at
looked
looking
looks
lose
lost
lot
love
lovely
lucky
lunch
machine
machines
made
magazines
main
mainly
make
makes
man
manager
manufacturing
many
mark
marks
marked
market
marketing
markets
married
match
matches
matter
May
me
meal
mean
meet
meeting
members
memo
men
mend
mended
mends
message
message pad
met
metal
metre
metres
mid-day
middle
midnight
mine
minister
Miss
mistake
mistakes
mobile
moment
Monday
money
month
more
morning
most
mother
movie
moving
Mr
Mrs
Ms
much
multiple
multiple choice
musical

musician
must
my
myself
name
names
national
near
nearest
nearly
need
needs
new
news
newspaper
next
next to
nice
night
nine
no
none
non-smoking
no-one
normally
north
not
nothing
now
number
o'clock

of
office
offices
Oh
old
older
oldest
on
one
only
open
opened
opposite
or
order
ordered
orders
other
our
out
outside
over
overcoat
own
owner
pad
paint
painter
painting
paints
paper

papers
park
parked
pay
pen
pencil
people
perhaps
person
personnel
phone
phoned
photocopier
photocopy
photocopying
picture
pictures
piece
place
plan
planned
plans
plant
plastic
play
played
playing
plays
please
pleased
pointing

Portugal
possible
post
pot
pounds
practice
prefer
present
price
Prime Minister
problem
problems
produced
product
project
provided
punctuation
put
putting
question
questions
queue
quiet
quite
railway
raining
rang
reach
read
reading
reads

ready
really
rearrange
receive
received
reception
receptionist
rectangular
remember
repair
repairman
repairs
report
required
rest
restaurant
return
returning
returns
right
ring
ringing
road
room
rooms
round
safe
said
sales
same
sandwich

sandwiches
saucer
saxophone
say
saying
says
scarf
school
Scotland
second
secretary
section
see
seeing
seems
sees
sell
sells
send
sent
sentence
sentences
seven
shade
shaking
shall
shape
she
she's
shelf
shelves

shirt
shop
shopping
shops
short
should
show
shown
side
silk
sir
sitting
six
sixteen
size
sky
sleep
sleeping
small
smaller
smallest
smoke
smoking
so
soft
sold
some
someone
something
son
soon

sorry
sound
south
Spain
Spanish
speak
speaking
speaks
spectacles
speedy
spelling
spell
spent
spoke
square
staff
staff room
stage
stairs
stand
standing
start
station
stay
still
stock
store
stores
strap
street
striped

student
studies
studying
successful
suitcase
suitcases
sunny
sure
Switzerland
table
tables
take
takes
taking
talk
talking
talks
tall
tallest
task
taxi
tea
teacher
teachers
team
teams
telephone
telephoned
telephones
telephoning
television

tell
telling
tells
ten
than
thank
thanks
that
that's
the
theatre
them
then
there
these
they
thing
things
think
thinks
third
thirteen
this
those
thousand
three
through
Thursday
tick
time
times

timetable
tired
to
today
together
told
tomorrow
tonight
too
top
total
tourists
towards
town
toy
traffic
train
trains
travel
travellers
tray
tree
trees
triangular
tried
true
try
Tuesday
TV
twelve
twenty

twice
two
type
umbrella
under
underneath
understand
understands
United Kingdom
until
upon
upset
urgently
us
use
used
using
van
various
vase
vegetables
very
view
visit
visited
visiting
visits
waiting
walking
wall
walls

want
wanted
wants
was
wasn’t
wastepaper
wastepaper bin
wastepaper basket
watch
water
way
we
we’d
wearing
weather
Wednesday
week
weeks
well
were
wet
what
what’s
when
where
which
while
who
who’s
why
wife
will
win
window
windows
wish
wishes
with
woman
women
won
won’t
wonderful
wood
words
work
worked
working
works
world
worry
worth
would
write
writes
writing
written
wrong
year
years
yes
yesterday
you
young
younger
your

Section	Examiner's Use Only
A	
B	
C	
Total	

SAMPLE EXAMINATION PAPER 2

LCCI EXAMINATIONS BOARD

ENGLISH FOR BUSINESS

PRELIMINARY LEVEL

(Code No: 1044)

Instructions to Candidates

(a) The time allowed for this examination is ***1½*** *hours.*

(b) Answer all **3** *sections.*

(c) Use the spaces provided in the combined question and answer booklet to complete the answers. If more space is needed for answers or rough notes, use the supplementary sheets provided and secure them inside your booklet with your name and candidate number clearly written on each sheet. Rough notes should be clearly crossed through.

(d) Credit will be given for correct spelling, punctuation and grammar.

(e) Adequate and appropriate communication is required rather than a particular number of words.

(f) When you finish, check your work carefully.

(g) The use of standard English dictionaries and cordless non-programmable calculators is permitted. Candidates whose first language is not English may use a bilingual dictionary.

ENTER DETAILS BELOW

CANDIDATE'S NAME IN FULL
as it is to appear on the certificate **IDENTITY CARD NUMBER** ....

Subject Code Number ....**1044**.................................

Candidate's Number .... Centre Code ....

Full Private Address ....

.... Postcode ....

Centre Name and Address ....

....

STATE HERE THE NUMBER OF ADDITIONAL SHEETS HANDED IN ☐

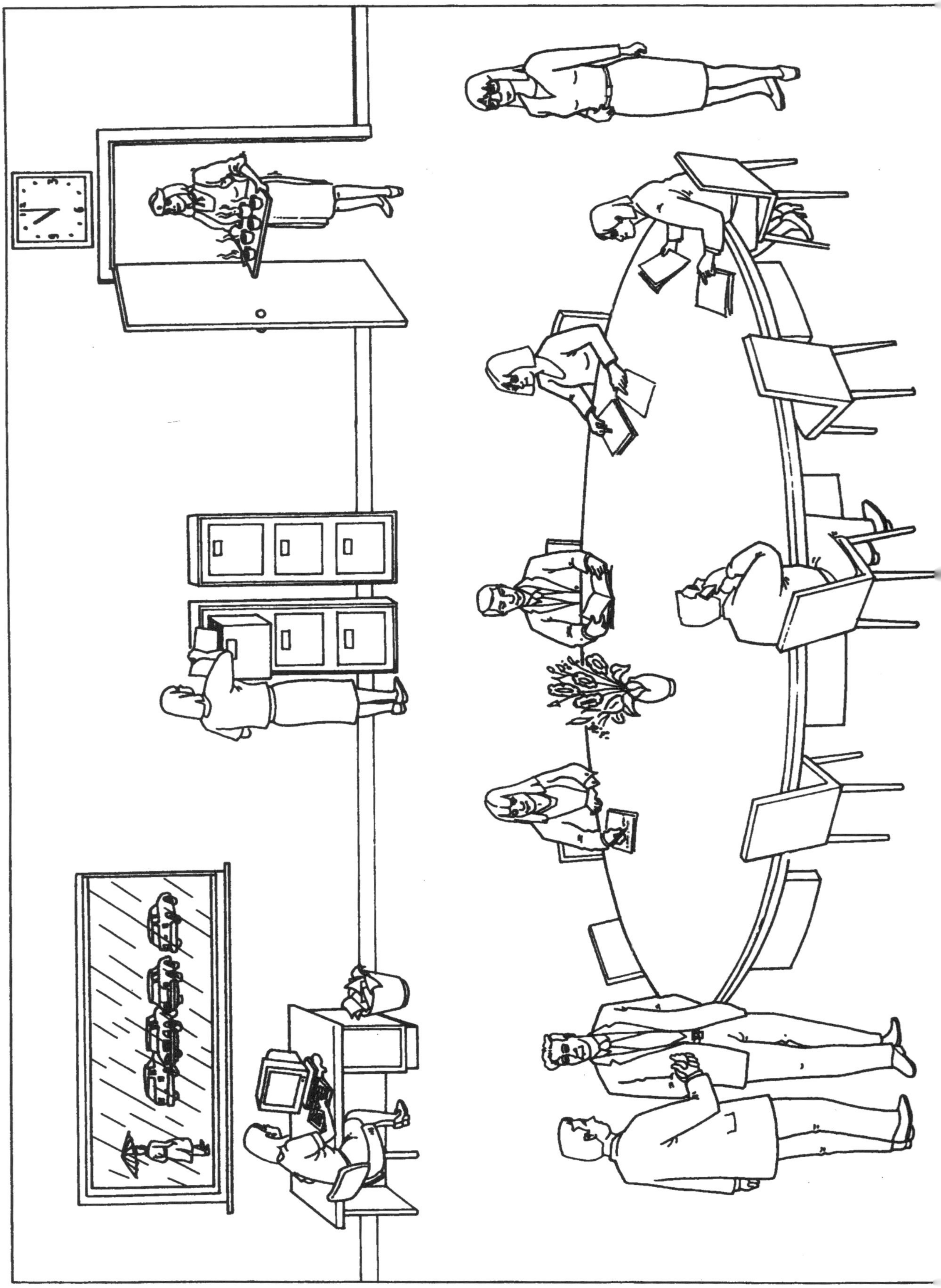

Section A

Look at the picture. Put a tick (✓) in the box for the best answer to each question.

A1 What is the picture? (1 mark)

(a) a dining room ☐

(b) a meeting room ☐

(c) a factory ☐

A2 How many people are sitting? (1 mark)

(a) none ☐

(b) six ☐

(c) five ☐

A3 What is in the middle of the large table? (1 mark)

(a) a vase of flowers ☐

(b) a pot of coffee ☐

(c) a computer ☐

A4 What can you see outside the window? (1 mark)

(a) a park ☐

(b) a car ☐

(c) a car park ☐

A5 What is between the window and the door? (1 mark)

(a) the clock ☐

(b) a desk ☐

(c) some filing cabinets ☐

A6 A woman has opened a drawer of a filing cabinet. Which one? (1 mark)

(a) the top drawer ☐

(b) the middle drawer ☐

(c) the bottom drawer ☐

CONTINUED ON NEXT PAGE

SECTION A CONTINUED

A7 Two men are standing near the big table. What are they doing? (1 mark)

(a) carrying a box ☐

(b) writing a letter ☐

(c) shaking hands ☐

A8 What is the woman wearing a hat bringing into the room? (1 mark)

(a) cups of tea and coffee ☐

(b) a briefcase ☐

(c) an umbrella ☐

A9 Where is the wastepaper bin? (1 mark)

(a) next to the round table ☐

(b) next to the square table ☐

(c) behind the window ☐

A10 A woman wearing spectacles is standing. Is she (1 mark)

(a) on the right of the picture? ☐

(b) on the left of the picture? ☐

(c) in the middle of the picture? ☐

A11 What is the big table made of? (1 mark)

(a) paper ☐

(b) leather ☐

(c) wood ☐

A12 Is the wastepaper bin? (1 mark)

(a) full? ☐

(b) empty? ☐

(c) open? ☐

SECTION A CONTINUED

A13 Which of these can you not see in the picture? (1 mark)

- (a) a mobile phone ☐
- (b) a computer ☐
- (c) a photocopy machine ☐

A14 A woman is writing with a pen. Where is she? (1 mark)

- (a) near the window ☐
- (b) next to the door ☐
- (c) at the big table ☐

A15 Which is the tallest? (1mark)

- (a) the big table ☐
- (b) the filing cabinets ☐
- (c) the small table ☐

Look at the picture. Then write short answers to these questions where it says Answer.

A16 How many chairs are empty? (2 marks)

Answer ______________________________

A17 Where is the clock? (2 marks)

Answer ______________________________

A18 What shape is the clock? (2 marks)

Answer ______________________________

A19 Who is talking on a mobile phone? (2 marks)

Answer ______________________________

A20 Is the door closed? (2 marks)

Answer ______________________________

A21 What time is it? (2 marks)

Answer ______________________________

A22 What is the weather like outside the room? (2 marks)

Answer ______________________________

CONTINUED ON NEXT PAGE

SECTION A CONTINUED

A23 A woman is sitting under the window. What is she doing? (2 marks)

Answer ______________________________

A24 Where is the person with an umbrella? (2 marks)

Answer ______________________________

A25 A man is sitting at the big table next to a woman who is writing. What is he doing? (2 marks)

Answer ______________________________

(Total 35 marks)

SECTION B

Karen Brown works in a bookshop called Notting Hill Books in London, United Kingdom. The shop sells books for travellers and tourists. People visit the shop to buy books and they can also telephone the shop to buy books.

Karen is now speaking on the telephone to a man called Gregory da Silva.

Karen: Notting Hill books, Karen Brown speaking. Can I help you?
Mr da Silva: Good morning, Karen. This is Gregory da Silva from Braga in Portugal. I have visited your shop before.
Karen: Hello, Mr da Silva. I remember you. You bought a lot of books about London when you visited our shop.
Mr da Silva: I did. I enjoyed my visit to London and the books helped me. In fact, I would like to buy some more. Can I order books over the telephone?
Karen: Yes. As you are a good customer we can send you the books and the bill.
Mr da Silva: Thank you. I am going to visit the North of England next month and I would like some books about the cities of this area. Do you have a book about the City of Durham?
Karen: Oh yes. We have an excellent book, "A Guide to Durham". It costs £15. Are you visiting other cities?
Mr da Silva: Yes. I am going to visit York and Newcastle upon Tyne.
Karen: They are both very interesting cities. We have a good guide to York which costs £20 and an excellent guide to Newcastle upon Tyne, with many pictures. This also costs £20.
Mr da Silva: I'll have those three books please. Could you send me the bill in euros? I prefer to pay in euros, not pounds.
Karen: Certainly. I will ask our Despatch Manager, Bruce Grant, to send you the books and a bill in euros. We have your address.
Mr da Silva: Thank you, Karen. I shall look forward to reading the books before I visit England again. I hope to return next year and perhaps visit Scotland.
Karen: I hope you enjoy your visit to England. Goodbye Mr da Silva.

Read these sentences about the conversation. Some are true and some are false. Put a tick (✓) in the TRUE or FALSE box.

		TRUE	FALSE	
B1	Karen Brown works in a bookshop.	☐	☐	(1 mark)
B2	Mr da Silva has visited Notting Hill Books before.	☐	☐	(1 mark)
B3	You can only buy books if you visit the shop.	☐	☐	(1 mark)
B4	Karen Brown answered the telephone.	☐	☐	(1 mark)

SECTION B CONTINUED

		TRUE	FALSE	
B5	Braga is in the United Kingdom.	☐	☐	(1 mark)
B6	Mr da Silva is going to visit London next month.	☐	☐	(1 mark)
B7	The book about Newcastle upon Tyne has many pictures.	☐	☐	(1 mark)
B8	Mr da Silva did not enjoy his visit to London.	☐	☐	(1 mark)
B9	The books on Durham, York and Newcastle upon Tyne are the same price.	☐	☐	(1 mark)
B10	Mr da Silva will read the books before he visits England.	☐	☐	(1 mark)
B11	Mr da Silva wants to pay for the books in pounds.	☐	☐	(1 mark)

Write a sentence to answer each question about the conversation on the line marked Answer.

B12 What time of day is it when Karen speaks to Mr da Silva? (3 marks)

Answer ______________________________

B13 What is Mr da Silva's first name? (3 marks)

Answer ______________________________

B14 What does Karen remember about Mr da Silva? (3 marks)

Answer ______________________________

B15 Where are the cities of Durham, York and Newcastle upon Tyne? (3 marks)

Answer ______________________________

B16 In which city does Mr da Silva live? (3 marks)

Answer ______________________________

B17 Who is Bruce Grant? (3 marks)

Answer ______________________________

B18 Where does Mr da Silva hope to visit next year? (3 marks)

Answer ______________________________

B19 What is the total cost of the books Mr da Silva wants to buy? (3 marks)

Answer ______________________________

(Total 35 marks)

OVER

SECTION C

Read the conversation again and then look at this table.

Pounds sterling	Euros
10	15.63
15	23.45
20	31.26
25	39.08
30	46.89
35	54.71
40	62.52
45	70.34
50	78.15
55	85.97
60	93.78

Use the information to work out the cost of the three books in euros. The books are called "A Guide to Durham", "A Guide to York" and "A Guide to Newcastle upon Tyne".

Then write a **memo** to Bruce Grant, the Despatch Manager, asking him to despatch the books as agreed in your conversation with Mr da Silva.

<u>MEMORANDUM</u>

To: ______________________________ Date: ________________

From: ____________________________

Subject: ____

(30 marks)

Answers: Sample Examination Paper 1

Section A

A1 (a)	A16 inside
A2 (b)	A17 on a desk
A3 (b)	A18 right hand
A4 (b)	A19 raining
A5 (c)	A20 open
A6 (a)	A21 three
A7 (c)	A22 women
A8 (a)	A23 reading a letter
A9 (a)	A24 the woman on the left
A10 (c)	A25 eight
A11 (a)	
A12 (c)	
A13 (b)	
A14 (a)	
A15 (b)	

Section B

B1	True	B12	It is morning.
B2	False	B13	She is the secretary of Speedy Repairs.
B3	True	B14	He was tall and wearing glasses.
B4	True	B15	He will be at work.
B5	True	B16	Their favourite movie is "Titanic".
B6	False	B17	She will be at home until 11.30.
B7	True	B18	It is based in Newbridge.
B8	False	B19	It has no picture.
B9	True		
B10	False		
B11	True		

Section C

MEMORANDUM

To: Pat Wagner   Date: Today's date

From: Karen Duval

Subject: Mr Singh

Mr Singh telephoned the office this morning.

You went to his house in 56 Central Drive yesterday because his television wasn't working. It had no sound and you mended it.

Mr Singh says it now has no picture. He was angry because he wanted to watch "Titanic" last night with his family.

Please can you visit his house tomorrow morning and mend his television. He is at work but his wife will be at home until 11.30.

Answers: Sample Examination Paper 2

Section A

A1 (b)
A2 (b)
A3 (a)
A4 (c)
A5 (c)
A6 (a)
A7 (c)
A8 (a)
A9 (b)
A10 (a)
A11 (c)
A12 (a)
A13 (c)
A14 (c)
A15 (b)
A16 three
A17 above the door
A18 square
A19 the man sitting at the front of the picture
A20 no
A21 eleven o'clock
A22 raining
A23 using a computer
A24 in the car park
A25 reading

Section B

B1 True
B2 True
B3 False
B4 True
B5 False
B6 False
B7 True
B8 False
B9 False
B10 True
B11 False
B12 She speaks to him in the morning.
B13 His first name is Gregory.
B14 She remembers that he bought a lot of books about London.
B15 They are in the North of England.
B16 He lives in Braga.
B17 He's the Despatch Manager at Notting Hill Books.
B18 He hopes to visit Scotland next year.
B19 The total cost is £55.00.

Section C

MEMORANDUM

To: Bruce Grant   Date: Today's date

From: Karen Brown

Subject: Order – Mr da Silva, Portugal

Mr Gregory da Silva from Portugal telephoned this morning. He ordered three books and wants the bill in Euros. The books are:

A Guide to Durham (€23.45)
A Guide to York (€31.26)
A Guide to Newcastle upon Tyne (€31.26)

Please send him the books and a bill in Euros. The total amount is €85.97. You have his address.